Betraying the National Interest

Betraying

Frances Moore Lappé
Rachel Schurman
Kevin Danaher

the National Interest

A Food First Book • **Grove Press** • NEW YORK

PUBLISHED BY GROVE PRESS, INC.
920 BROADWAY
NEW YORK, N.Y. 10010

LIBRARY OF CONGRESS CATALOGING-IN-PUBLICATION DATA
LAPPÉ, FRANCES MOORE.
    BETRAYING THE NATIONAL INTEREST.
    "A FOOD FIRST BOOK."
    BIBLIOGRAPHY: P.
    I. ECONOMIC ASSISTANCE—DEVELOPING COUNTRIES.
I. SCHURMAN, RACHEL. II. DANAHER, KEVIN. III. TITLE.
HC60.L325 1987 338.91 87-12067
ISBN 0-8021-0012-0
ISBN 0-8021-3027-5 (pbk.)

MANUFACTURED IN THE UNITED STATES OF AMERICA
FIRST EDITION 1987

10 9 8 7 6 5 4 3 2 1

For my father, whose critical openness to new ideas
has inspired me for a lifetime.

F.M.L.

For my father, from whom I inherited my values, convictions,
and thirst for social justice.

R.S.

For my brother, James Danaher.

K.D.

Acknowledgments

OUR GREATEST DEBT is to Jessica Pitt, whose excellent research assistance contributed immeasurably to the quality of this book and whose enthusiasm lightened the labor. Our thanks also to two other Institute interns—Chris Benner and Lee Saffron—for their help on the project.

A number of our colleagues at the Institute contributed generously of their time to improve the manuscript and prepare it for publication: Walden Bello, Medea Benjamin, Rebecca Buell, Jon Christensen, Joe Collins, Alan Epstein, Andrea Freedman, Ann Kelly, and Audee Kochiyama-Holman.

Others outside the Institute offered invaluable feedback to our work in progress: David Beckmann, Steve Commins, Eva Gold, Guy Gran, Tony Jackson, David Kinley, Carl Mabbs-Zeno, Russell Middleton, Sara Miles, Bill Rau, and Jane Slaughter. Walt Bode of Grove Press contributed excellent editing assistance. To each of you, our heartfelt thanks.

We also relied on many government officials and information specialists who generously shared their time and expertise with us. While many may prefer to remain unnamed, their help has not gone unappreciated.

Our final debt of gratitude goes to the thousands of Institute members. Without your constant encouragement and support, this book—like all of our Institute's work—would not have been possible. Thank you.

Contents

List of Charts

Betraying the National Interest

Foreign Aid and the National Interest

DESPITE THE GENEROSITY and goodwill of most Americans, U.S. foreign aid isn't working. If its goal is to alleviate poverty abroad, we search in vain for evidence of its success. Among major recipients of U.S. aid—the Philippines, India, and Central American nations, for example—the number of people living in poverty has climbed as foreign aid has increased. Even government-sponsored studies admit that many of the best-sounding projects to help the poorest people often fail to reach them.

If, on the other hand, the goal of U.S. aid is to heighten national security by stabilizing foreign governments and tying them more closely to us, then it is also failing. Since the early 1970s, many of the U.S. government's long-standing allies into which it plowed billions of dollars in aid have fallen— including the Shah of Iran, Somoza of Nicaragua, Marcos of the Philippines, and Haile Selassie in Ethiopia.[1] Others—par-

---

1. Others include Lon Nol of Cambodia (now Kampuchea), Thieu of South Vietnam, Tolbert of Liberia, Duvalier of Haiti, and Numieri of Sudan.

3

ticularly those mentioned in this book: Pakistan, Zaire, Honduras, El Salvador—now have little or no more popular support than did those deposed regimes.

But our goal is not simply to decry foreign aid's failures. It is to find out *why* it fails. In even setting out on such a search, however, we face a major obstacle: a worn-out, stale debate lies waiting to trap us.

On one side are those who decry U.S. aid's stinginess, pointing out—correctly—that the United States provides a lower percentage of its Gross National Product (GNP) in foreign aid than any other western nation. More substantively, they call for the United States to reform its aid program, shifting its focus from *our* military-dominated security interests to *others'* humanitarian concerns. Foreign aid should be an expression of our generosity, not a weapon of influence or war.

On the other side, many argue that sentiment mixed into the art of statecraft can be dangerous. Given real-world geopolitics, we cannot afford to let humanitarian concerns dictate the distribution of our aid. America has a lot to offer other nations, they maintain, but we will have nothing to give if we don't look out for ourselves first. This means using foreign aid as a deliberate arm of foreign policy to keep friendly governments in power. It also means using aid to influence others toward specific policies favorable to us.

In bare outline, these positions define the debate. Unfortunately, they also limit it by encouraging us to ask the wrong questions. How can we reform aid so that it serves the interests of the poor abroad instead of U.S. interests? Or, how can we use aid more effectively as a weapon to keep governments in power which pledge allegiance to the United States?

The very premises of both positions are flawed. The humanitarians opt for concern for others, while the realists would put us first. But we suggest—being unflinchingly realistic—that it is impossible to divide these interests. Even to see the possibility, however, of constructing a foreign aid policy on the basis of common interests takes some hard thinking.

One must consider just *what are* the needs of the majority of people now poor, hungry, and illiterate in the third world. What is the root of their poverty and what is necessary to overcome it?

In previous books, notably *Food First: Beyond the Myth of Scarcity* [2] and *World Hunger: Twelve Myths*, [3] we have tried carefully to document how people are made hungry. In virtually every country, either current production or yet untapped local potential could meet the needs of the entire people. Thus, too many people or the unfortunate calamities of nature do not cause hunger. Hunger is human-made. It occurs where economic and political rules and institutions have so constricted control over farmland and other basic resources that some people are left with no power at all, not even to secure their most elementary human needs.

If this analysis of the social roots of hunger—now broadly accepted [4]—is true, then hunger cannot be addressed except through far-reaching change, change which shifts power to those who now have none. This is the first interest of the poor and hungry—an interest in society-wide change toward more dispersed, more democratic access to resources.

But what of ourselves? What are *our* overriding interests? High on the list is economic security—the need for remunerative and reliable work. As our economy becomes increasingly dominated by globe-spanning corporations in the 1980s, it is clearer than ever that poverty in the third world directly threatens that interest. As long as workers there are prevented from organizing to protect their interests, U.S. wages and jobs are jeopardized by American companies relocating to low-

---

2. Frances Moore Lappé and Joseph Collins with Cary Fowler, *Food First: Beyond the Myth of Scarcity* (New York: Ballantine, 1979).

3. Frances Moore Lappé and Joseph Collins, *World Hunger: Twelve Myths* (San Francisco and New York: Food First Books/Grove Press, 1986).

4. Even the World Bank acknowledges that the main cause of hunger is poverty and the human institutions that perpetuate it. See *Poverty and Hunger: Issues and Options for Food Security in Developing Countries* (Washington, D.C.: World Bank, 1986).

wage havens abroad. Moreover, if third-world people are kept too poor to buy even basic goods, much less amenities, U.S. producers are denied many millions of third-world customers.

There is a further, more subtle threat. In third-world societies where the majority are too poor to buy the products produced in their own fields and factories, large growers, businesspeople, and governments will increasingly orient production toward export markets. Without customers at home, no local market can be profitable enough for them. This intensified push to export will continue to undercut markets for U.S. producers, especially those of American farmers.

Beyond our economic well-being, Americans have an interest in physical security, a need to defuse an increasingly volatile world—four times as many people have been killed in wars and other civil conflicts during the forty years since World War II as in the forty years preceding it.[5] Just as with economic security, we contend that the legitimate interest of Americans in reduced violence cannot be achieved as long as half the world's people are deprived of life's essentials. As long as people are made to go hungry, the level of conflict in the world can only rise.

Bluntly stated, it takes violence to keep people hungry. People do not continue watching loved ones die needlessly of hunger. They resist. In many countries, religious movements stressing innate human rights fortify their demands: "As a child of God," a Nicaraguan peasant leader told us, "I learned that I have the right to live and that means the right to have land so that my family won't starve." No amount of U.S. military aid used to suppress them will convince the poor to acquiesce. "I stand for peace," this peasant told us, "but not peace with hunger."

Thus, even if we could live with ourselves in a world increasingly split between surfeit and hunger, we would also

---

5. Ruth Leger Sivard, *World Military and Social Expenditures 1985* (Washington D.C.: World Priorities, 1985), 9.

have to live with greater instability, with more resources poured into military interventions in the third world. And we would have to live with the resulting hostility from those who see their rights denied with the assistance of U.S. weapons. National security based on fear of change inevitably means less and less security for us.

From this perspective, seeing the unity—or at least the over-lapping—of interests appears not only possible but crucial. Both they *and* we would gain from far-reaching change in many third-world countries, where resources are today so tightly held.

AID AND A POLICY OF FEAR

For the most part, however, those defining U.S. national security since World War II have perceived our interests very differently. To them, our national interest is an ideological and military victory over a "red menace," or, more recently, an "evil empire." From their vantage point, any serious movement for change in the third world threatens the United States in two ways: first, the political opening that such change entails provides room for the Soviet Union to gain influence; second, any change that addresses the roots of hunger must have economic restructuring high on its agenda—democratizing control of land, credit, the national budget, and so on. U.S. policymakers have labeled any such agenda a "communist threat" because it inevitably challenges the sanctity of the market and the prerogatives of wealth.

To U.S. policymakers, our world is divided sharply between "us" and "them." There are only two camps. From the 1954 U.S.-assisted overthrow of a reform government in Guatemala, to the assassination of the Congo's Patrice Lumumba in 1965, to covert war against the Nicaraguan government in the 1980s, U.S. policymakers have perceived virtually any nation to be in the opposing, Soviet camp if it challenges the economic rules we take for granted and is not actively allied to the United States. Defense Department official Noel Koch put it this way:

> Whatever the non-aligned, Third World nations like to think, the world is really divided in two—not three: countries that are communist and countries that aren't. . . . So we really face a larger version of the question put in Lincoln's time, and it is whether the world can exist half slave and half free.[6]

In the view of Washington, the United States must beat back the "expansionist and destabilizing behavior of the Soviet Union" virtually alone.[7]

Because so much hinges on these crucial assumptions—that no nation can be independent of control by one or the other superpower, and growing Soviet expansionism threatens the third world—we devote an entire chapter to them. Chapter 6 examines the record of Soviet involvement in the third world.

The rest of our book focuses on just how this definition of the national interest, one that automatically construes far-reaching change as a threat to U.S. interests, subverts the potentially positive contribution of U.S. foreign aid programs.

AN AID POLICY BLINDED BY DOGMA

This book examines U.S. bilateral aid, that is, aid flowing directly from the United States to governments abroad. We have chosen this focus, excluding the much smaller portion of U.S. aid flowing through multilateral institutions—such as the World Bank and U.N. agencies—because the United States controls bilateral assistance directly. Therefore, it is the clearest indicator of the goals and priorities of U.S. foreign policy.

---

6. Koch was then overseer of U.S. Special Operations Forces. Speech inserted into the *Congressional Record*. Apr. 3, 1984, S3660.

7. U.S. Agency for International Development, *Congressional Presentation for Security Assistance Programs. Fiscal Year 1987*. vol. 1, 9.

Most U.S. bilateral foreign aid is of three types (See Chart 1), but its priorities are abundantly clear in the concentration of our aid dollars. With both economic and military components, security assistance now comprises two-thirds of U.S. foreign aid, and is the fastest growing part. Security assistance makes no pretense of targeting the needs of the poor. Its purpose is to "stem the spread of economic and political disruption and to help allies in dealing with threats to their security and independence."[8] So explains the Agency for International Development (AID) responsible for implementing most U.S. aid programs. Our government's own rhetoric

CHART 1: DISTRIBUTION OF U.S. BILATERAL AID, 1981–1986 (COMBINED)

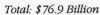

Total: $76.9 Billion

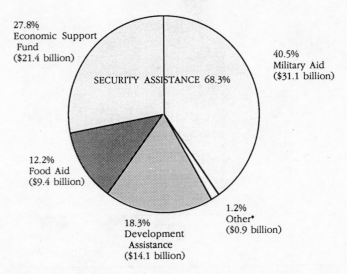

27.8%
Economic Support
Fund
($21.4 billion)

SECURITY ASSISTANCE 68.3%

40.5%
Military Aid
($31.1 billion)

12.2%
Food Aid
($9.4 billion)

1.2%
Other*
($0.9 billion)

18.3%
Development
Assistance
($14.1 billion)

*Peace Corps and narcotics

Sources: For 1981–85, U.S. Agency for International Development, *U.S. Overseas Loans and Grants,* various years; for 1986, AID *Congressional Presentation, Fiscal Year 1988,* main vol., 868.

---

8. AID, *Congressional Presentation. FY 1987.* main vol., 99.

is thus clear on this point: security assistance is to help protect the status quo.

Chapter 1 highlights how Economic Support Funds (ESF) serve this function. Growing eighty-four percent in real terms between 1981 and 1986 (see Chart 2), less than ten percent of U.S. tax dollars transferred abroad under this program goes to countries designated "low income" by the World Bank. Forty-two percent goes to countries considered "upper mid-

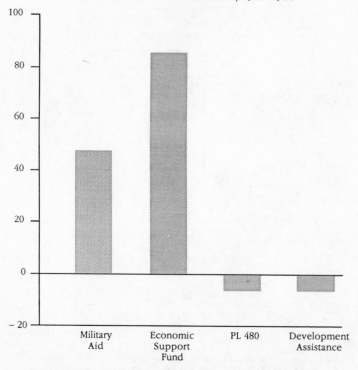

CHART 2: PERCENT CHANGE IN REAL SPENDING
ON FOUR U.S. AID PROGRAMS, 1981–1986*

*Adjusted for inflation using the Bureau of Labor Statistics Consumer Price Index

Sources: For 1981–85, U.S. Agency for International Development, *U.S. Overseas Loans and Grants,* July 15, 1945–Sept. 30, 1985; for 1986, AID *Congressional Presentation, Fiscal Year 1988,* main vol., 868.

dle income." Not only is the direction of ESF support unrelated to the poverty of the recipient, but it rewards many
antidemocratic regimes actively resisting reforms that might
allow our aid to benefit the poor. Theoretically, ESF is the
economic as opposed to military arm of security assistance. But
chapters 1 and 2 show how easily economic aid becomes just
another arm of U.S. military assistance.

Chapter 2 explores the biggest component of U.S. foreign
aid—military assistance. Swelling forty-eight percent during
the first half of the eighties, military assistance now comprises
forty-one percent of all our aid.[9] U.S. military aid, we have
learned, is not just about shipping arms abroad. It is integrated
into a comprehensive U.S. strategy—largely unseen by the
American people—to intimidate dissidents and to quell insurgencies against third-world governments that the United
States deems its allies. The militarization of foreign aid is a key
element in a wider pattern of growing military dominance of
foreign policy. Unable to grasp the roots of rebellion against
the status quo in the third world, Washington uses our aid
dollars in a futile effort to stave off that resistance. Throughout
our book, we suggest that such attempts to solve social problems with military strategy not only fail but backfire.

While security assistance has been growing, the remaining
programs—development assistance, and food aid—have di-
minished. They now comprise eighteen and twelve percent of
our aid respectively. Though their impact is therefore smaller,
their function is still eye-opening. In chapter 3 we suggest that
while U.S. development assistance may appear more effective
in addressing third-world poverty than the hard-nosed approach of security assistance, it is nonetheless stymied by the
same internal contradiction. Even the best-intended project

---

9. As our book was going to press in late 1986, Congress cut foreign aid by about
eight percent, trimming military aid by fourteen percent. These cuts did not emerge,
however, from public or congressional protest over the types of critical issues raised
here. Pushed by the Gramm-Rudman-Hollings legislation, Congress was simply slash-
ing those budget items—like foreign aid—least likely to bring them political repercus-
sions. Despite these cuts, the thrust of our foreign aid policies remains unchanged.

cannot touch the root of rural people's hunger and poverty if it is unable to challenge the structure of control over resources that impoverished them to begin with. Similarly, food aid appears to most Americans as the unmitigated good counterbalancing military aid. Yet evidence in chapter 4 suggests that most food aid flows as another means of budgetary support for favored U.S. allies. And food aid, it turns out, has additional drawbacks as a tool for positive change abroad.

Exploring U.S. development assistance and food aid pushes us to think critically about the very meaning of development itself—and how and by whom it can be achieved. Moreover, understanding both programs is vital to grasping how our government views our interests.

ECONOMIC DOGMA AND FOREIGN AID

Our government's view of the world as a battleground between "them" and "us" not only contributes to a military-dominated foreign policy but powerfully shapes the content of the strictly economic portion of U.S. foreign aid. Washington believes that any economic system not like ours, must be like theirs. Economies are either capitalist or communist. Thus, the United States must use its foreign aid program as a lever to reform third-world economies—to make them more open to foreign investment and market-oriented like ours. The buzz-word is privatization—reducing the government's role in the economy. Increasingly, U.S. aid to third-world governments is awarded on the basis of just such "policy reforms."

In many cases, basic economic reform is needed—badly needed. But, as we will see in chapter 5, Washington's dogmatic stance prevents it from seeing that the prerequisites for the success of its economic formula simply do not exist in many third-world countries. How can the magic of the marketplace, for example, work to end hunger if the customers are missing—that is, if people are too poor to be part of the market?

How can private enterprise free people from hunger in the third world if private capital is actually fleeing Africa and Latin America in search of surer investments elsewhere?

FOREIGN AID BUILT ON COMMON GROUND

Thus, we are not suggesting that a reform of foreign aid requires selfless humanitarianism. It demands something more profound: *that as Americans we reconceive our national interest.* Could we as a people come to see that the challenge of effective foreign aid is not to advance the interests of the poor abroad over those of Americans, or vice versa? Could we come to perceive the unity of interests of most Americans with those who are made to go hungry in the third world?

In the second half of the 1980s, surely the deepening suffering and growing violence in the third world suggest that the postwar keep-the-lid-on-change stance of our foreign aid policies needs reappraisal. The stakes are high. Once U.S. foreign policy, and in particular U.S. foreign aid, is narrowly predicated on a Soviet expansionist threat, virtually any action by our government is justified—no matter how it violates American democratic values or counters the needs of the hungry for change. Surely we cut our own throats when we allow our government to side with elites against the demands of the poor or engage in state terrorism against poor countries. Such policies undermine U.S. credibility throughout the world and threaten to drive third-world peoples to the Soviets for their very survival. More subtle, but equally central to our well-being, such an approach to foreign aid necessitates heightened government secrecy, undermining the very democracy it claims to be defending.

Our book is thus an indictment of U.S. foreign aid, but not merely to elicit outrage. We wrote this book to help Americans see behind the reassuring rhetoric and official rationales in order to understand *why* it is failing. Once the false premises of U.S. policies are understood, we believe Americans will perceive U.S. foreign aid as nothing less than a betrayal of the national interest. And with this insight, they will be prepared to undertake the profound rethinking of our real interests that must precede a redirection of U.S. aid programs.

One

Security Aid:
But Who's More Secure?

THE FASTEST GROWING PART of U.S. foreign aid is also
the least visible. How many Americans have even *heard* of
Economic Support Funds (ESF)? No doubt very few, yet ESF
loans and grants to foreign governments now make up over
one-quarter of all U.S. aid, about $4.9 billion in 1986.[1]

The State Department makes no bones about ESF's objectives. They are "to support U.S. economic, political and security interests and the advancement of U.S. foreign policy
objectives." This means, in Washington's view, shoring up
threatened allies: "These funds provide the resources
needed . . . to stem the spread of economic and political
disruption and to help allies in dealing with threats to their
security and independence," explains the State Department.[2]

Between 1981 and 1986, tax dollars going to ESF grew

---

1. Calculated from U.S. Agency for International Development, *Congressional Presentation, Fiscal Year 1988,* main vol., 868.

2. AID, *Congressional Presentation, FY 1987,* main vol., 99.

eighty-four percent in real terms (see Chart 2), and the number of recipient countries more than doubled—jumping from twenty in 1981 to fifty-two in 1986.[3] About two-thirds of ESF aid is simply a cash transfer—money the United States gives or loans to a foreign government to keep it financially solvent. Such cash payments help the recipient government pay for imports and interest on the national debt. The biggest recipients appear in Chart 3. Most of the rest goes toward projects in recipient countries.[4] But unlike those funded under the U.S. development assistance pro-

CHART 3: TOP TEN RECIPIENTS OF U.S. ECONOMIC SUPPORT FUNDS (ESF) 1981–1986
($ millions)

Country	ESF $
1. Israel	$7,113.5
2. Egypt	$5,299.3
3. Turkey	$1,218.1
*4. Pakistan	$964.2
5. El Salvador	$822.2
6. Costa Rica	$587.6
*7. Sudan	$526.0
8. Philippines	$439.6
9. Jamaica	$363.9
10. Honduras	$341.5

*Countries designated low-income by the World Bank, *World Development Report 1985*

Source: U.S. Agency for International Development, *Congressional Presentation, Fiscal Years 1983–1987.*

---

3. Calculated from AID, *Congressional Presentation, FY 1983,* main vol., 481–484, and *Congressional Presentation, FY 1988,* main vol., 870–872.

4. About one-quarter goes to specific projects. A final tenth of ESF assistance goes to promote U.S. exports. Under what is called the Commodity Import Program, governments get foreign exchange to import specific U.S. goods and services. For more background on ESF, see U.S. General Accounting Office, *Political and Economic Factors Influencing Economic Support Fund Programs,* report no. GAO/ID-83-43 (Washington, D.C.: U.S. GAO, Apr. 18, 1983).

gram we discuss in chapter 3, ESF projects scarcely pretend to target the poor.[5] Most are high-visibility projects, designed as public symbols of U.S. government support.[6] In the Philippines, for instance, nearly two-thirds of ESF project aid in the early eighties went to build roads, schools, and the like, near U.S. military facilities. The U.S. government's General Accounting Office explains the rationale: in part to make "Filipinos aware of the economic benefits derived from continued U.S. use of the bases."[7]

The biggest beneficiaries of ESF are in the Middle East. During the first six years of the 1980s, over $12 billion in ESF flowed to Israel and Egypt alone. Together they receive about one-quarter of all such monies. The rationale behind this massive, ongoing aid is no mystery—to keep U.S. friends in power in a region of vital strategic importance. Aid to Egypt is that country's payoff for its separate peace with Israel at Camp David in 1979.

So singlemindedly fixed on keeping these governments afloat, U.S. aid exceeds even the recipient's capacity to use it effectively. In Egypt, for example, U.S. taxpayers are spending over a billion ESF dollars to overhaul Cairo's sewer system. It's a huge "white elephant," an AID official told us and predicted that without the necessary bureaucracy to operate and maintain it, the project will be a gigantic waste of money. But, he stressed, U.S. corporations selling equipment for the project will profit anyway.[8]

In theory, Economic Support Funds go with some strings

---

5. The U.S. law stipulates that ESF be directed, "to the maximum extent possible," toward meeting basic human needs, but, as this chapter demonstrates, that "maximum extent" turns out to be quite minimal.

6. See, for instance, GAO, *Political and Economic Factors Influencing Economic Support Fund Programs.* Also: John W. Sewell and Christine Contee, "U.S. Foreign Aid in the 1980s," in John W. Sewell et al., *U.S. Foreign Policy and the Third World: Agenda 1985–1986* (New Brunswick, N.J.: Transaction Books, 1985), 102.

7. GAO, *Economic Support Fund Assistance to the Philippines,* report no. GAO/NSIAD-84-44 (Washington, D.C.: U.S. GAO, Jan. 27, 1984), 7.

8. IFDP telephone interview, Nov. 1986. The official prefers not to be identified. Egypt is the second largest recipient of U.S. aid after Israel. Aid *Congressional Presentation, FY 1986,* Near East vol., 40.

attached—they are not to be used for military purposes. In reality, once ESF dollars are transferred to the recipient government's bank, AID's "financial controls cease," notes the General Accounting Office.[9] All of Israel's ESF aid—$1.9 billion in 1986—is a cash transfer. Most ends up as interest payments on Israel's huge foreign debt, largely owed to U.S. banks for military purchases.[10] ESF aid to Israel thus becomes additional military aid by another name. "A virtual blank check," is what the United States provides to Israel, observed former Assistant Secretary of State Harold Saunders in 1986.[11] What Saunders calls this "mindlessly close" relationship—because it avoids tough policy questions—may well be making Middle East peace even more unattainable. Confident it has the United States' unconditional support, the Israeli government has less incentive to negotiate a settlement with its Arab neighbors.

Our billions in open-ended aid to Egypt and Israel have also allowed both to continue along paths to economic disaster. One of the world's largest foreign debtors, Egypt must now import half its food. Besides U.S. aid, money sent home by expatriate workers is about all that keeps the economy afloat. In Israel, inflation has hit 100 percent every year since 1979 and in 1984 approached 1000 percent.[12] Heavy overseas borrowing to support large government expenditures—mainly on

---

9. A 1984 GAO report describes the problem of simply keeping track of the money: "The AID cash transfer payment procedure . . . begins with U.S. dollars being electronically transferred directly to a recipient government's bank account where they are commingled with funds from other sources." See GAO, *U.S. Economic Assistance to Central America.* report no. GAO/NSIAD-84-71, (Washington, D.C.: U.S. GAO, Mar. 8, 1984), 3.

10. "The American Survey: Time to Put Paid to AID," *The Economist,* Apr. 6, 1985, 21.

11. Charles R. Babcock, "The U.S. and Israel Are Closer Than Ever," *The Washington Post National Weekly Edition.* Aug. 18, 1986, 7.

12. "Uncle Sam's Widening Role in the Israeli Economy," *Business Week.* Oct. 29, 1984, 42. Although it appears that Israel's hyperinflation—with a 100,000% increase in consumer prices between 1979 and 1985—has finally been brought under control as of mid-1986, it was only through a sizeable cut in real wages and an increase in unemployment that this slowdown was achieved. See "Inflation Is Down, But Not Out," *The Economist.* July 12, 1986, 69.

the military—has saddled the country with the highest per person foreign debt in the world.[13]

ESF largesse for Egypt and Israel reflects one aspect of our government's policy, the notion that simply transferring billions year after year can buy influence and stability. Certainly, it has not bought internal economic stability; and regional stability is as remote as ever. The primary focus of our book, however, is not the Middle East; it is an exploration of the impact of U.S. aid to the third world. Let us now turn to that central concern.

KEEPING THE LID ON CHANGE

Above we noted that ESF's stated purpose is to assist countries of "particular strategic or political importance to the United States."[14] But which countries are of such importance?

To U.S. policymakers, they are any which serve to obstruct the spread of communism. And which are these? Those permitting U.S. military installations and activities overseas and those willing to facilitate U.S. access to raw materials. Ultimately, however, they include any country which agrees to be counted in the U.S. camp. Its government may be resisting internal change simply to protect its own privileges, but a cry of communist threat ensures U.S. support.

It's no surprise, then, that the poverty of the recipient nation is not a consideration in disbursing the ESF. More critical, neither is the recipient government's accountability to its people.

The Philippines. Despite Ferdinand Marcos's long record as a cruel dictator, U.S. aid not only continued but increased.[15]

---

13. In 1986, the total Israeli debt was $24 billion, or about $5,700 per capita. See "Israel's Economy," *The Economist* July 12, 1986, 69–71.

14. AID, *Congressional Presentation FY 1986,* main vol., 94.

15. Aid to the Philippines jumped fifty-five percent between 1971 and 1972 (from $58.2 million to $90.5 million). It has continued on this steady incline ever since. Between 1972 and 1985, the United States gave Marcos $390 million in ESF and $689 million in military aid.

Between its declaration of martial law in 1972 and 1985, the Marcos government received over a billion dollars in ESF and military aid. And in 1983, President Reagan pledged almost $1 billion more aid over the next five years.[16] In the eyes of American officials, only continued support for Marcos assured U.S. access to Clark Air Base and Subic Naval Base, both deemed essential to U.S. national security.

Are these bases really essential to our security? Without them, the United States would still have 92,000 land troops, thirty-two bases and the Seventh Fleet at sea in East Asia and the Pacific.[17] In the view of many military and political experts, the Philippine bases are convenient but not necessary. Even the architect of containment strategy and former ambassador to the Soviet Union, George Kennan, had concluded by 1977:

> The original justification for the maintenance of these bases has now been extensively undermined. . . . The American response . . . should be, surely, the immediate, complete, absolute and wordless withdrawal of the facilities and equipment they contain, leaving the Philippine government the real estate and only that.[18]

Moreover, the bases represent multiple problems in relations between the two countries. Opposition to the bases among Filipinos is long-standing, born at the turn of the century when 125,000 U.S. troops were sent to quell a revolt by Filipinos opposed to U.S. colonial rule. As early as the 1940s, Dwight D. Eisenhower recognized the U.S. bases as a hindrance to the development of sound relations between the two countries.[19] The bases also make more likely increased U.S. involvement in the Philippine government's counterinsur-

---

16. "U.S. Bases in the Philippines: Assets or Liabilities?" *The Defense Monitor,* vol. 15, no. 4, 1986, 7. Published by the Center for Defense Information, the directors of which include six retired military officers.

17. Ibid., 1.

18. George Kennan, *The Cloud of Danger* (Boston: Little, Brown, 1977), 97–98.

19. "U.S. Bases in the Philippines," 1.

gency warfare. Such ties could well place U.S. troops at risk, bringing the type of involvement the United States now has in Central American internal conflicts.

Neither U.S. interests, nor the interests of the vast majority of Filipinos are served by letting the fear of losing the bases dictate the type of government the United States will support. The heavy price of our government's long backing of Marcos should make this point clear. Consider the legacy the new government must now overcome: while Marcos amassed a personal financial empire, real wages fell, export crops replaced food crops and Filipinos became among the worst fed people in Asia. In 1986, the World Bank estimated that the Philippines' per capita Gross National Product was below what it was a decade ago. Even with high growth, per capita consumption cannot soon recover—even to those earlier poverty levels. Since a mere tenth of the population has been allowed to take control over eighty percent of the wealth, far-reaching reforms will have to succeed before any overall growth will help the millions of hungry Filipinos.[20]

Liberia.   Turning to Africa, the second largest recipient of ESF funds on the continent is Liberia, founded by freed American slaves in 1822. Despite protests against widespread government human rights abuses, within four years of a military takeover by Sergeant Samuel Doe, U.S. aid had jumped tenfold.[21]

Justifying our mounting aid, U.S. officials have praised Liberia's political progress. In 1985, U.S. Assistant Secretary of State for Africa, Chester Crocker, described Liberia's election approvingly as an "imperfect beginning" of a "democratic experience."[22] By that time Doe had already executed more

---

20. Mark Fineman, "Economic Woes in the Philippines," *San Francisco Chronicle*, May 28, 1986, F5. Fineman's statistics come from studies performed by the World Bank.

21. AID, *Congressional Presentation, FY 1987*, main vol., 666.

22. Chester A. Crocker, "Recent Developments in Liberia," statement before the Subcommittee on African Affairs of the Senate Foreign Relations Committee, Dec. 10, 1985. *Current Policy*, no. 772, U.S. Department of State, Washington, D.C.

people than all his predecessors combined,[23] and his election had been widely discredited within Liberia as rigged. In early 1987, when Secretary of State George Shultz visited Liberia and lauded its "progress," particularly its freedom of the press, several censored opposition Liberian journalists expressed amazement.[24] Can U.S. credibility withstand public portrayals of our allies that "seem to be flying in the face of fact," as one silenced Liberia journalist put it?

Doe's rule has done little to gain him the confidence of his people. While U.S. aid makes up one-third of the nation's budget, the poor majority gain little: Liberia's health statistics remain among the worst in the world, and eighty percent of the people are illiterate.[25] Rushing to defend himself to a questioner, Doe protested that he had done a lot for the people, "a lot of things which I cannot recall now."[26]

Fear of the Soviets is not a plausible justification for abiding U.S. support for such a government. To gain a foothold, the Soviets would have to undo centuries-old cultural and economic links between Liberia and the United States. Liberia's first constitution was written at Harvard Law School, the U.S. dollar is legal tender, and U.S. corporations—particularly Firestone rubber—are vital to its economy.[27] Moreover, shoring up Doe out of fear of losing a site for our military communications station or the Voice of America transmitting station now located in Liberia may be similarly ill-reasoned. In the long run, is our national interest really served? "What Americans are doing will create a lot of anti-American feeling in the country," warned a Liberian journalist, angered by

---

23. Ernest Harsch, "A Dictatorship Propped Up by Washington," *Intercontinental Press*, Apr. 21, 1986, 251.

24. *The New York Times*, Jan. 16, 1987, 1, 3.

25. Health statistics are from the World Bank, *World Development Report, 1985*, table 23.

26. Michael Massing, "How Liberia Held 'Free' Elections," *The Nation*, Jan. 25, 1986, 71.

27. Ibid., 74.

Secretary Shultz's praise for his country's repressive government.

Zaire.　Since coming to power in 1965, Mobutu Sese Seko has been "our man" in Central Africa—receiving $844 million in U.S. aid, of which $147 million has come from the ESF.[28] Much of Mobutu's personal wealth—estimated at between $4 and $5 billion[29]—is believed to have come from Zaire's national treasury and from kickbacks from the foreign companies mining Zaire's minerals. Despite its stunning natural wealth, Zaire remains the fifth "poorest" nation in the world according to the World Bank. Malnutrition takes the lives of more than one-third of Zaire's citizens.[30]

Mobutu has ruled Zaire (formerly the Belgian Congo) since 1965, when a CIA-engineered coup assassinated Patrice Lumumba, head of the country's first elected government.[31] The United States feared Lumumba was moving toward socialism, and, thus, U.S. companies would be deprived of Zaire's precious cobalt, copper, and diamonds.

But in his revealing book, *Endless Enemies,* veteran *Wall Street Journal* reporter Jonathan Kwitny questions whether under Lumumba Zaire was, indeed, headed towards socialism. "In fact, all through his brief career as a leader [Lumumba] pledged to respect private property and even foreign investment," writes Kwitny.[32] Even if Kwitny were wrong, does it follow that a socialist Zaire would have ended the West's

28. In 1982, the U.S. House Foreign Affairs Committee did vote to cut Zaire's military sales credits by eighty percent and to veto a proposed $15 million in ESF support. Despite this show of discontent, U.S. aid continued and in 1986 reached $76 million, more than double the level of the early 1980s.

29. "Zaire: Mobutu's $4 Billion Stash," *The Nation,* Feb. 26, 1983, 230.

30. Jonathan Kwitny, *Endless Enemies: The Making of an Unfriendly World* (New York: Congdon and Weed, 1984), 10. Malnutrition figures come from a survey conducted in 1980 by a team that included members of the U.S. Peace Corps.

31. Ibid., 54.

32. Ibid., 72. Kwitny's highly readable account is not limited to Zaire, but covers the U.S.'s role in other countries as well.

access to Zaire's valuable minerals? The intervening years have seen the United States trading with many socialist countries, including the People's Republic of China—in 1986 we even sold subsidized wheat to the Soviets! When socialist Kwame Nkrumah governed Ghana (1960–1966), the United States continued to trade our goods for Ghanaian cocoa. Today, the United States is Marxist Angola's biggest trading partner, and U.S. commerce continues with socialist-led Zimbabwe. As with the Philippines under Marcos, or Liberia under Doe, the rationale for U.S. support for Mobutu's repressive government is neither cogent nor consistent.

Pakistan. Pakistan is the fourth largest recipient of Economic Support Funds. Since President Zia ul-Haq seized power in a 1977 military coup, nearly half of all government expenditures have been for the armed forces.[33] Without ESF assistance, could the Zia regime have afforded such a diversion of the national budget?

In 1985, while proposing $329 million in economic aid to Zia's government,[34] the U.S. State Department admitted in its annual human rights report: "There are frequent and credible allegations of police, paramilitary, and military torture of detainees" in Pakistan.[35] Zia has suspended the constitution and kept educational institutions under tight control.[36] Nevertheless, strong diplomatic support continues. In 1985, on a trip to Pakistan, Henry Kissinger paid tribute to the country as a "front-line state" in defense of "free people" everywhere. A leading Zia opponent shot back: "People who are denied

---

33. "Please Forget the Past," *The Economist.* Oct. 12, 1985, 47.

34. Proposed for fiscal year 1986. AID, *Congressional Presentation. FY 1986.* main vol., 674.

35. "Country Reports on Human Rights Practices for 1984," report submitted to the Senate Committee on Foreign Relations and the House Committee on Foreign Affairs by the Department of State, Feb. 1985, 1361.

36. Charles Lister, "America Can Help Pakistan Avoid Violence—Or Worse," *The Los Angeles Times.* Dec. 26, 1984, pt. 2, 5.

human rights in their own country can hardly be expected to do much for other people's freedom."[37]

U.S. support for General Zia is officially defended on the grounds that Pakistan is a bulwark against further Soviet influence in South and Southwest Asia.[38] But, as with the Philippines or Zaire, would a U.S. refusal to bankroll a repressive government necessarily lead to a pro-Soviet one?

The actual Soviet record in that region suggests that the U.S.S.R. has for some years been seeking a negotiated settlement with Pakistan's neighbor, Afghanistan, indicating that Soviet leadership may now see its occupation of that country as a costly mistake.[39] Furthermore, Soviet involvement in the region has not always resulted in anti-American governments. The Soviet Union has provided over $14 billion in economic and military aid to India since 1955, yet India is considered a U.S. ally.[40]

Central America. According to studies cited by the Kissinger Commission, between one-half and three-quarters of the people of El Salvador, Honduras, Guatemala, and Nicaragua "could not satisfy their basic needs in terms of nutrition, housing, health and education" during the 1970s.[41] And in each of these countries, poverty has only deepened in the intervening years. In El Salvador, land ownership is so skewed that six wealthy families control as much farmland as 300,000 peasants.

37. Aslam Khan, "Zia's 'Islamic Democracy' Leading Pakistan into the Past," *The Nation.* June 29, 1985, 794.

38. U.S. Department of State, *Congressional Presentation for Security Assistance Programs. FY 1987.* vol. 1, 41.

39. See, for example, Lawrence Lifschultz, "Can the Pieces Fit Into Place?" *The Nation.* May 31, 1986, 751–756.

40. "Soviet Geopolitical Momentum: Myth or Menace? Trends of Soviet Influence Around the World from 1945 to 1986," *The Defense Monitor.* Center for Defense Information, vol. 15, no. 5, 1986, 23.

41. "Report of the National Bipartisan Commission on Central America," Jan. 1984, 24.

Any reforms that attacked the roots of such life-destroying imbalances would have to be sweeping. But Washington, arguing that any political opening necessary to pursue such reforms would also allow increased Soviet influence, is determined to keep the lid on at all costs. Just since 1980, ESF aid to Central America has climbed forty-fourfold, reaching $437 million in 1986.[42] In the following chapter we describe how the ESF has become an invisible form of military aid to governments fighting internal uprisings. By 1987, the government of El Salvador alone will have received well over a billion ESF dollars along with hundreds of millions more in direct military aid.

As long as the U.S. government refuses to recognize that third-world nations might seek to be independent of both the United States and the Soviet Union, it is bound—out of fear of Soviet influence—to be used by the most unsavory despots. The governments we highlight in this chapter are only a sampling. Ultimately, however, a foreign policy based on fear becomes self-fulfilling, as U.S. actions alienate millions of people abroad whose interests are hurt by the tyrants it supports. This inevitability becomes even clearer when we consider the role of U.S. military assistance, now the largest chunk of our foreign aid.

---

42. ESF aid to Central America was $10 million in 1980. AID, *Congressional Presentation. FY 1988.* main vol., 872. In 1985, ESF aid to Central America was even higher—$736 million, Ibid., FY 1987, 668.

Two

Armed Aid: At War With American Values

ALWAYS A SUBSTANTIAL PART of the U.S. foreign aid program, the military's share of the aid pie grew from thirty-four percent to forty percent of our aid budget during the first half of the 1980s.[1] At $5.8 billion, military aid now represents two-and-one-half times what is spent on development projects and over three times what is spent on food aid.[2] (The accompanying box describes the three primary U.S. military aid programs in brief.)

The Reagan administration's emphasis on military aid becomes strikingly clear when we look at aid to Sub-Saharan Africa. During the first four years of the Reagan administration, military aid nearly doubled while development assistance rose only seventeen percent.[3] In Latin America and the Carib-

---

1. U.S. Agency for International Development, *Congressional Presentation, Fiscal Year 1988,* main vol., 868.

2. Development assistance in 1986 was $2.3 billion and food aid, $1.7 billion. Ibid.

3. Nominal dollars. Military aid increased by ninety-eight percent between 1981 and 1985. Calculations based on "actual" expenditures taken from AID, *Congressional*

U.S. Military Aid Programs: An Overview

The U.S. military aid program has three main components, each with a slightly different function. Many countries receive more than one type of military aid.

Foreign Military Sales Program: FMS provides loans and grants to foreign governments to purchase U.S. military arms and training. It accounts for the lion's share of U.S. military aid—over eighty-five percent in 1986. Although most FMS credits are offered at market rates of interest, concessional loans have become increasingly common in recent years.

Military Assistance Program: MAP accounted for about fourteen percent of military assistance in 1986. It, too, provides funds for the purchase of American-made arms, but unlike FMS, MAP consists of grants instead of loans. Major MAP recipients in the first half of the 1980s include Turkey, Portugal, El Salvador, and Honduras. New countries slated to receive MAP grants in 1987 are the Central African Republic, Colombia, Ecuador, Guatemala, and Uruguay.

International Military Education and Training Program: IMET is used to provide military training to foreign armed forces. Despite its small size, IMET reaches a great many countries. In 1986, for instance, eighty-five different countries received this form of military aid. The State Department estimates that during the last thirty-five years, IMET has provided training to over 500,000 military personnel in more than 100 countries.

CHART 4: MILITARY ASSISTANCE
Composition of U.S. Military Aid Program, 1986

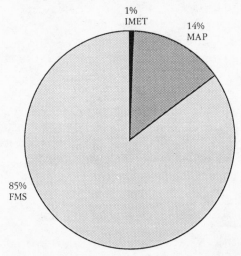

1%
IMET

14%
MAP

85%
FMS

Source: U.S. Agency for International Development, *Congressional Presentation, Fiscal Year 1988*, main vol., 868.

bean, the trend is even more pronounced. There, U.S. military assistance jumped *fourfold* to $238 million between 1981 and 1986.[4]

And that's just overt aid. Adding covert aid would make the increase sharper still. *Newsweek* estimated that in the summer of 1986, as Congress approved $100 million for the contras to overthrow Nicaragua's government, the CIA was actually preparing to provide them with support equivalent to $400 million.[5] At the time of this writing, the tangled web of covert aid flowing at Washington's behest from foreign governments and private parties through Swiss bank accounts to the contras had still not been sorted out. But the disclosures give credence to those who have charged that the American Congress has been allowed to vote only on the tip of an iceberg that is increasingly covert.

While spending for military assistance has climbed markedly, so have the number of recipients. In the first six years of the 1980s, the number of governments receiving U.S. military aid increased from fifty-seven to eighty-nine.[6] Among the new recruits are a large number of African governments, almost doubling to thirty-four since 1980.

A FOOT IN THE DOOR

Many new recipients of U.S. military aid receive only small amounts of assistance (on the order of $1 million or less), often in the form of training under the International Military Education and Training program (IMET). But it's usually only a matter of time before other kinds of U.S. military aid begin to flow. In its 1987 Presentation to Congress, the Department of State described what happened in the case of El Salvador:

Presentation, FY 1983 and 1987, main vol. In 1986, development assistance was $378.9 million while military assistance was $103.2 million.

4. Data are for fiscal years. In 1981 military assistance was $60 million. AID, *Congressional Presentation, FY 1983 and 1988.*

5. "Rekindling the Magic," *Newsweek,* July 7, 1986.

6. AID, *Congressional Presentation, FY 1983 and 1988,* main vol.

Military assistance to El Salvador necessarily began with basic infantry equipment and training. Then, the U.S. provided transport vehicles, medical equipment, and training and larger caliber arms. From there, we expanded to communications in an integrated command, control and communications system, and to a logistics and maintenance infrastructure. All capabilities had to be developed by a step-by-step process.[7]

El Salvador received only $600,000 in military aid in 1970; by 1986 this sum had leapt over *two hundredfold* to reach $122 million.[8]

ARMED AGAINST WHOM?

To understand the impact of increased U.S. military aid requires that we look at what kinds of governments the United States chooses to arm. Many face no external threat; they need arms to intimidate their own people. A quantitative analysis of U.S. foreign aid to Latin America in the 1970s, for example, found a uniformly positive correlation between U.S. aid and human rights violations.[9] In other words, governments receiving U.S. support were more likely to violate their people's human rights.

In 1985, as many as forty-three of the 113 countries receiving U.S. military or security aid were under some form of military rule.[10] In fact, during the last twenty years, the United States has given over $27 billion in arms to military-domi-

---

7. AID, *Congressional Presentation for Security Assistance Programs, FY 1987.* vol. 1, 19.

8. AID, *Congressional Presentation. FY 1988.* main vol., 872.

9. Lars Schoultz, "U.S. Foreign Policy and Human Rights Violations in Latin America: A Comparative Analysis of Foreign Aid Distributions," *Comparative Politics.* Jan. 1981, 162.

10. Calculated based on data presented in Ruth Leger Sivard, *World Military and Social Expenditures 1985* (Washington, D.C.: World Priorities, 1985), 24; and AID, *Congressional Presentation. FY 1987.* main vol., 666–668 (AID data refer to 1985.)

CHART 5: TOP TEN RECIPIENTS OF U.S. MILITARY
ASSISTANCE 1981–1986
($ millions)

Country	Military Assistance $
1. Israel	$9,322.6
2. Egypt	6,569.2
3. Turkey	3,098.8
4. Greece	2,175.3
5. Spain	1,846.7
6. Pakistan	1,200.1
7. South Korea	1,145.1
8. El Salvador	658.4
9. Portugal	579.6
10. Thailand	522.5

Source: U.S. Agency for International Development, *Congressional Presentation. Fiscal Years 1983–1987.* main vols.

nated governments where government violence against citizens is all too common.[11] Military-controlled governments are three times more likely to use torture than other third-world countries, notes Ruth Leger Sivard, a leading authority on world military expenditures.[12] Sivard's findings are reinforced by our compilation in Chart 6, showing that twenty-six of the forty-three military-controlled governments now or recently receiving U.S. aid have frequently committed acts of violence against their people. The list includes a host of infamous dictators, from the deposed Baby Doc Duvalier of Haiti to Mobutu Sese Seko of Zaire.

U.S. military aid can also abet the military's drive to domi-

---

11. Dee Anne Dodd, "The Militarization of Foreign Aid," *American Friends Service Committee,* 1984, 2. Edward Herman (*CovertAction,* no. 26, 30) reports that between 1950 and 1979, military aid programs transferred $107.3 billion in arms and ammunitions to U.S. clients.

12. Sivard, *World Military and Social Expenditures 1985* (Washington, D.C.: World Priorities, 1985), 19.

CHART 6: U.S. FOREIGN AID TO
MILITARY-CONTROLLED GOVERNMENTS (1985)

Country	Economic Assistance	Military Assistance	Frequent Official Violence Against Citizens
AFRICA			
Benin	*	*	
Burkina Faso	*	*	
Burundi	*	*	
Central African Republic	*	*	*
Chad	*	*	*
Congo	*		
Eq. Guinea	*	*†	
Ethiopia	*		*
Ghana	*	*	*
Guinea	*	*	*
Liberia	*	*	*
Madagascar	*	*	
Malawi	*	*	*
Mali	*	*	*
Mauritania	*	*	*
Niger	*	*	
Rwanda	*	*†	
Somalia	*	*	*
Sudan	*	*	
Togo	*	*†	*
Uganda	*	*†	
Zaire	*	*	*
ASIA/NEAR EAST			
Afghanistan	*		*
Algeria		*†	
Bangladesh	*	*	*
Burma	*	*	
Indonesia	*	*	*
Jordan	*	*	

CHART 6: *(Continued)*

Country	Economic Assistance	Military Assistance	Frequent Official Violence Against Citizens
Korea (South)		*	*
Lebanon	*	*	
Pakistan	*	*	*
Philippines	*	*	*
Thailand	*	*	
Turkey	*	*	*
Yemen	*	*	
LATIN AMERICA & CARIBBEAN			
Colombia		*	*
El Salvador	*	*	*
Guatemala	*	*	*
Haiti	*	*	*
Honduras	*	*	*
Panama	*	*	
Paraguay	*	*	*
Peru	*	*	*

†Received $50,000 or less.

Source: U.S. Agency For International Development, *Congressional Presentation. Fiscal Year 1987.* 666–668, and Ruth Leger Sivard, *World Military and Social Expenditures 1985* (Washington, D.C.: World Priorities, 1985), 24.

nate civilian institutions. With U.S. help, the number of Philippine military personnel climbed fivefold after the imposition of martial law. A Filipina described their penetration throughout her society:

> In 1972, when Martial Law was declared, we had 50,000 military personnel. Now we have more than 250,000, as well as several paramilitary units. Whereas the military

used to be confined to security affairs, now you will find military men in the judicial, legislative, administrative and executive bodies. . . . They arbitrarily pick people up and kill them. They go inside barrios, ransack houses and take whatever they can.[13]

Ferdinand Marcos was only too eager for U.S. military aid. But in some cases, Washington has even pushed military aid on reluctant governments. When civilian President Vinicio Cerezo of Guatemala took office in 1985, he bluntly asked President Reagan to delay offering military aid. He wanted first to gain control of the army—one of the most brutal in Latin America.[14] Despite Cerezo's plea for patience, the administration charged ahead, requesting from Congress $10.3 million in military assistance for Guatemala.[15]

Costa Rica's experience also suggests that Washington will push its arms agenda, regardless of the priorities of the recipient government. Historically, Costa Rica has been proud of its neutrality (disbanding its army in 1949). But in order to receive U.S. aid, it has been pressured to cooperate with U.S. military plans, making way for U.S. aircraft, military personnel, and a Voice of America relay station.[16] "In 1984 Costa Rica asked the United States to help modernize its police forces," reported one former Costa Rican official. "We requested $2 million . . . [but] we ended up with $7 or $8

13. Report from the Philippine Women's group, GABRIELA, at the Forum, Nairobi, Kenya, Aug. 1985. Reprinted in *Connexions* 17–18, Summer/Fall 1985, 53.

14. Shirley Christian, "New Guatemalan Leader Wary on U.S. Military Aid," *The New York Times*, Dec. 18, 1985, 8.

15. Ibid. According to some reports, Cerezo has been so pressured by the U.S. government that he has recently begun asking for military aid. (Source wishes to remain anonymous.) Certification necessary to receive U.S. aid was officially granted in mid-1986.

16. For more detail, see Eva Gold, "The U.S. Military Encirclement of Nicaragua," in *Reagan and the Sandinistas: The Undeclared War on Nicaragua*, ed. Thomas Walker (Boulder, Col.: Westview Press, 1987). Also available in reprint form from the American Friends Service Committee, 1501 Cherry St., Philadelphia, Penn. 19102.

million."[17] Costa Rica's dependence on the United States for economic support, amounting in 1986 to nearly half a million dollars *a day,* makes it hard for the government to refuse military-related aid.

THE ARMS BURDEN

By far the biggest chunk of the U.S. military aid budget goes to what's called Foreign Military Sales (FMS): U.S. government loans and/or grants for the purchase of U.S.-made military equipment. (See Chart 4.) Loans are long-term, often carrying lower-than-commercial rates. With such easy credit, many governments are quick to sign up.

The problems arise when these loans come due—as they have in a number of very poor countries.[18] Because the debts must be paid back in appreciated currencies—currencies worth more upon repayment than when the debt was incurred—they often end up costing the government far more than it had bargained for.[19] Public money which could theoretically be used for health care, education, or local development gets siphoned off to repay the loans.

Access to plenty of "easy-credit or grant military aid [helps] skew internal decision-making in favor of larger military expenditures," says Interfaith Action for Economic Justice, a group of religious agencies involved with development.[20] Even free military aid (a grant rather than a loan) can divert

---

17. Tina Rosenberg, "Costa Rica's Dilemma Over Aid," *San Francisco Chronicle,* May 7, 1986, F5.

18. According to *Business Week,* the countries facing the greatest debt repayment problems include Egypt, Turkey, Pakistan, Morocco, Somalia, Sudan, Tunisia, Zaire, and Israel. See "Arms Sales Turn Into Gifts for Struggling Third World Nations," *Business Week,* July 25, 1983, 63.

19. Because a number of key countries are having trouble repaying their FMS loans, the U.S. government has started to shift to outright grants. In the special cases of Israel and Egypt, loans valued at over $6 billion (accumulated over ten years) are being forgiven. See "Arms Sales Turn Into Gifts," 63.

20. Interfaith Action for Economic Justice, testimony before the House Subcommittee on Appropriations, May 17, 1985.

resources because there are always hidden costs. Building military-related infrastructure, such as airstrips or storage facilities, requires money to import spare parts and to train troops to use the imported equipment.

Honduras dramatizes the heavy drag which militarization places on an economy. Since 1982, the United States has swamped Honduras with military aid—building or improving nine combat airfields, two radar stations, and air intelligence installations.[21] Between 1980 and 1985, the size of the Honduran military doubled.[22] Despite U.S. aid, the cost to Honduras of all these "improvements" has been enormous. "Debt obligations, defense spending and declining tax revenues created a fiscal deficit of almost $300 million in 1983," reports the U.S. General Accounting Office. "As a result, resources have not been available to the Honduran government to accelerate improvements in living standards."[23]

MILITARY AID AND A STRATEGY OF INVISIBLE WAR

To grasp fully the danger in the growth of military assistance, we must step back for a moment.[24] We must try to see the world through the eyes of U.S. military strategists. To them, U.S. national interests lie not just in protecting our own borders or even in controlling key strategic points around the globe. When asked what areas of the world the Reagan administration would stress in reasserting U.S. influence, Secretary of Defense Caspar Weinberger responded: "All of

---

21. "U.S. Aid to Plan a Long Presence in Honduran Bases," *The New York Times*, July 13, 1986.

22. Central America Research Institute, "Five Years of Civilian Government," *Central America Bulletin*. vol. 4, no. 12, Oct. 1985, 7.

23. "Providing Effective Economic Assistance to El Salvador and Honduras: A Formidable Task," U.S. General Accounting Office, report no. GAO/NSIAD-85-82, (Washington D.C.: U.S. GAO, July 3, 1985), 27.

24. The following section benefited from the excellent research on low intensity conflict of Sara Miles and Tom Barry. See specific footnotes for their contributions.

them."[25] The goal is not peaceful coexistence with the Soviet Union, nor even containment. The Reagan administration is putting into place "a global offensive against communism at the fringes of the Soviet Empire," in the words of Secretary of State George Shultz.[26] A government specialist in national defense put it bluntly in testimony before the House Subcommittee on Foreign Relations:

> The principal focus of military assistance as military assistance has shifted. The programs began as a means to deter Soviet expansionism. Today they are primarily intended to deter or defeat aggression and subversion by *Soviet surrogates or that of other unfriendly states having their own agenda.* [emphasis ours][27]

In other words, just about any government whose agenda the United States decides it does not like is now fair game. The goal of this offensive is threefold: to tie anticommunist third-world governments ever more closely to the United States; to undercut popular uprisings in these countries; and to overthrow, or at least cripple, third-world governments unwilling to bow to U.S. hegemony. To carry out this global offensive, a counterinsurgency strategy is taking shape, now with a brand new label: low intensity conflict. It incorporates key lessons from Vietnam.

First, the experience of Vietnam taught U.S. militarists that Americans will not tolerate major loss of American lives in faraway battles against threats they don't themselves feel. So

---

25. Tom Barry, *Low Intensity Conflict: The New Battlefield in Central America,* The Resource Center, Box 4506, Albuquerque, N.M. 87196, 3, quoting *The Wall Street Journal,* Feb. 10, 1983.

26. Speech by George P. Shultz to the San Francisco Commonwealth Club, "America and the Struggle For Freedom," Feb. 22, 1985.

27. "Overview of Military Assistance Programs," statement of Richard F. Grimmett, Specialist in National Defense, Foreign Affairs and National Defense Division, before the Subcommittee on Foreign Operations, Committee on Appropriations, U.S. House of Representatives, Mar. 26, 1985, 9–10.

the new strategy for victory over global communism strives to avoid loss of U.S. lives. In this way, the war can proceed relatively unseen. More bluntly, low intensity conflict is a way for military planners to pursue their ends without the support of the American people. It is "a pseudonym for a war without full political support . . ." writes Lieutenant Colonel Richard Brawn in *Military Review.* [28] If low intensity conflict is successful, the American people will not even know we're at war.

Second, the emerging military consensus is that Vietnam did not prove the inadequacy of counterinsurgency warfare. It was never fully tested, say its advocates today. "The concept actually worked quite well in Vietnam," wrote Army Lt. Col. James A. Taylor in 1985. "But it was not seen that way by those who were so busy with quantifiable activities."[29] In his view, the Vietnam War was lost because General Westmoreland stuck stubbornly to conventional warfare, relying on heavy units, massive firepower, high-tech, and airpower.

The Reagan administration absorbed these lessons well: in the 1980s, counterinsurgency warfare has been resuscitated and developed into a full-blown, coordinated strategy.

Secrecy is a key to carrying out this low-profile war. This helps to explain why the CIA's annual budget—now $25 billion—has come to dwarf the amount allotted to overt foreign aid. It is three times what it was just one decade ago. At about forty a year, covert actions are currently at twice the level of the Carter years.[30] In 1986, the former chairman of the Intelligence Oversight Board, Thomas Farmer, noted that even in the earliest days of the Reagan administration, he detected a "tendency to substitute covert operations for foreign policy."

---

28. *Military Review,* Mar. 1985, quoted in Barry, *Low Intensity Conflict,* 16.

29. Sara Miles, "The Real War: Low Intensity Conflict in Central America," *Report on the Americas,* North American Congress on Latin America, 151 West 19th St., 9th fl., New York, N.Y. 10011, 22, quoting "Military Medicine's Expanding Role in Low-Intensity Conflict," *Military Medicine* Apr. 1985, 33.

30. Leslie Gelb, "Overseeing of CIA Has Produced Decade of Support," *The New York Times,* July 7, 1986, 1.

To him, their level and intensity seemed more appropriate to war than to peace.[31] Farmer expressed surprise, perhaps, only because he did not fully appreciate that Washington *is* at war.

To grasp the meaning of that war, in the remainder of this chapter we focus on Central America, in part because low-intensity-conflict strategists see the region as their laboratory. But covert U.S. aid in support of low-intensity wars now flows to Africa and Asia as well. Hundreds of millions of dollars in U.S. aid to Afghan rebels is by far the largest and most widely known example of the latter. In 1985 Congress also approved $5 million for the Khmer People's National Liberation Front and a group led by Prince Sihanouk. Both belong to a coalition including the Khmer Rouge,[32] which under Pol Pot was responsible for one of the most hideous atrocities of modern times: the deaths of over two million Cambodians.[33] At least $30 million in covert U.S. aid has gone to South Africa-backed Angolan rebels,[34] helping to perpetuate a war that is devastating Angola's economy. Once a net food exporter, Angola now survives on food aid, as farmers abandon fields in which the rebels have planted land mines. Hundreds of thousands of Angolans now face growing hunger and twenty to thirty percent of the children in conflicted areas are seriously malnourished.[35]

---

31. Daniel Schorr interview on National Public Radio, Dec. 13, 1986. Farmer was chairman of the Intelligence Oversight Board under Carter, and during the first six months of the Reagan administration.

32. Barbara Crossette, "Rift Seen in Cambodia Guerrilla Force," *The New York Times,* Dec. 23, 1985, 3.

33. Shirley Christian, "On Cambodia's Border, Shultz Visits Refugees," *The New York Times,* July 10, 1985, 4.

34. James Brooke, "U.S. Arms Airlift to Angola Rebels Is Said to Go On," *The New York Times,* July 27, 1987, 1.

35. Sheila Rule, "Toll of War: Angola's Mire Deepens," *The New York Times,* Sept. 19, 1986.

MILITARY, BUT BY MANY NAMES

More than a narrow—largely invisible—military strategy, low intensity conflict stresses the need to weave military action into economic, humanitarian, and psychological offensives.

U.S. aid programs to El Salvador illustrate how this weaving goes on. It begins with a request to Congress for economic aid that in reality ends up supporting specific military objectives. A 1985 study of aid to El Salvador sponsored by a congressional study group found that while the Reagan administration claimed economic aid to El Salvador was three times larger than military aid, the reverse was closer to the truth.[36] Of $1.7 billion in U.S. aid to El Salvador—$340 for every Salvadoran—during the first half of the 1980s, *seventy-four percent went in direct or indirect support of the government's war against a civil uprising.* Very little went to reform-oriented or development-oriented programs to remove the underlying causes of the war.[37]

In addition to the equivalent of $50,000 in direct U.S. military aid per enemy soldier, more than half a billion dollars in ESF cash transfers have gone to stave off the economic collapse of the Salvadoran government so that it could carry out the war, according to the report. "Without the Cash Transfer," the report concluded, "the Salvadoran Government could never have tripled its spending on the Armed Forces."[38]

A WAR FOR "HEARTS AND MINDS"

Central to this U.S.-sponsored war effort is what's been known since the Vietnam War as pacification. In part, pacification is pretty much as it sounds. A parent offers a pacifier when trying

36. *U.S. Aid to El Salvador: An Evaluation of the Past, A Proposal for the Future.* a report to the Arms Control and Foreign Policy Caucus, Jim Leach, Chairman, Feb. 1985. See also: *Help or Hindrance? United States Economic Aid in Central America* (San Francisco: Institute for Food and Development Policy, 1987).

37. Ibid., sec. 2.

38. Ibid., 18.

to quiet an infant *without* offering what it really wants. Government pacification efforts seek to woo people to its side without altering the root of their misery: elite control over land and other essential resources. But if that effort fails, the government will try to control people through intimidation.

Pacification highlights a key feature of low intensity conflict: *its target is not territory, but people*—to win the "hearts and minds" of the populace, as the U.S. military failed to do in Vietnam. Through giveaways and with propaganda, the government seeks to convince its citizens of its goodwill and its opponents' evil. But where a government is known for beating, torturing, raping, and killing tens of thousands of civilians—as in several Central American countries—this image reconstruction is a tall order indeed.

How to create a benevolent image for a government long associated with state terror? To low-intensity-conflict strategists, the answer is publicly linking the military with local civic improvement projects, food giveaways, and short-term medical assistance, as well as involving military personnel in youth and other civilian organizations. Longtime investigator of U.S. policies in Central America, Tom Barry, describes how such civic action works in El Salvador:

> When the Salvadoran Army rolls into a village, it is prepared to give a show. Planes drop propaganda leaflets on the area, and the commander presents a speech about the evils of communism and the virtues of the current regime. Food, toys, medicine, and clothing are handed out to villagers gathered in the plaza. Some battalions have their own soldier/clowns who provide entertainment. Frequently it becomes a multi-media affair when the army PSYOPS (Psychological Operations) team presents an anticommunist film from the United States. Army barbers cut hair, doctors give vaccinations, and dentists pull teeth.[39]

---

39. Barry, *Low Intensity Conflict*, 53.

Low intensity conflict also involves painting the U.S. military as a friend of the poor. In 1986, Dr. Richard Garfield, of Columbia University's School of Public Health, investigated the U.S. military's civic action program in Honduras. As part of U.S. military training exercises, soldiers go into tiny rural villages twice a week with four-ton mobile hospitals, replete with high-tech equipment. Their major activity is providing medicines to get rid of worms and other common afflictions. Yet these military medical forays cost the American taxpayer as much as $18,000 a day. "The purpose is to build good will—and apparently they are very successful," notes Garfield. "The villagers love the medicine, and they don't much care where it comes from."[40] Other observers are more doubtful. Two American Friends Service Committee investigators report that peasants bitterly criticize the civic actions as "purely propaganda," as they "don't address any of the causal issues, like lack of access to potable water and lack of ongoing medical attention."[41]

But pacification does not mean allowing the people to decide whether the government has more to offer than the rebels. It aggressively separates the populace from rebel forces. To help identify the enemy, pacification means making territory uninhabitable where rebels are thought to be active.

In support of the air war driving peasants out of the areas controlled by the rebels, U.S. funds for military aircraft for El Salvador jumped sevenfold between 1983 and 1984.[42] Fleeing peasants become refugees whom the government then tries to resettle under its control. As a result of the war, one-fifth of the population has already been forced to abandon

---

40. IFDP interview, June 1986.

41. Eva Gold and Mary Day Kent, "The Ahuas Tara II Exercises," a supplement to *A View of the U.S. Role in the Militarization of Central America,* based on a trip to Central America from Nov. 20, 1983 to Dec. 14, 1983, 2–3, NARMIC/AFSC, 1501 Cherry St., Philadelphia, Penn. 19102.

42. *U.S. Aid to El Salvador,* fig. 2, 15.

their homes, a higher percentage than in Vietnam at the height of the war.[43]

Pacification also involves civil defense, defined by a U.S. Embassy spokesman in El Salvador as a way of mobilizing the population in a "political statement of support for the government."[44] Ideally, all able-bodied men in a village are registered to serve in a militia to guard against rebel attack. Those unwilling to serve or who don't show up are marked as rebel sympathizers. In El Salvador, peasants typically are told that if they don't sign up for civil defense they can't expect more civic actions like the medical help described above.[45]

In Guatemala civil defense goes much further: as many as 75,000 peasants have been moved into what the army calls model villages.[46] In these Vietnam-style "strategic hamlets," people's freedom of movement is restricted. Not only are all adult men required to serve in the civil patrols, they may also be called to provide unpaid labor for the military.[47]

Propaganda is equally important to a "hearts and minds" war strategy. An anticommunist lecture is just as much part of a civic action as the free medicine. And official graffiti is a constant reminder that low intensity conflict must control how people interpret the world. In El Salvador the highway is lined with such slogans as: "Thank you for supporting democracy." But mass media are even more important. At least fifteen Honduran journalists are on the CIA payroll, former leader among the Nicaraguan contras, Edgar Chamorro, told

43. Ibid., 18–19.

44. Eva Gold, "The New Face of War in El Salvador: A View of Counterinsurgency Warfare," NARMIC, American Friends Service Committee, 1501 Cherry St., Philadelphia, Penn. 19102, Feb. 1986, 5.

45. Ibid., 5–6.

46. Chris Krueger and Kjell Enge, *Security and Development Conditions in the Guatemalan Highlands,* Washington Office on Latin America, 1985, v. An excellent report on village programs in Guatemala.

47. "Guatemala: A Human Rights Tragedy," NISGUA, 930 F St. NW, Rm. 515, Washington, D.C. 20004, 3. For background, see: "Civil Patrols in Guatemala," an Americas Watch Report, Americas Watch, 705 G St. SE, Washington, D.C. 20003.

the International Court of Justice in 1985. They are paid to speak favorably about the contras and call for the overthrow of the Nicaraguan government.[48] Similarly, in Costa Rica, U.S. funds pay for newspaper ads to turn Costa Ricans against Nicaragua, portraying it as a godless, totalitarian state.[49]

PUTTING ON A CIVILIAN FACE

Beyond the battlefield, beyond the countryside and the barrio, low intensity conflict targets the highest levels of government in what its designers term "nation building." The U.S. Congress is more likely to vote aid for elected governments than for military dictatorships.[50] Thus, the goal of "militarizing civilian life at the grassroots," that we've just described, is combined with "civilianizing the government at the national level," writes low-intensity-conflict investigator Sara Miles.[51] The $2 million in clandestine U.S. funds to help elect José Napoleón Duarte in El Salvador were thus part of a coherent strategy. With his election, U.S. officials could ignore the fact that hundreds of opposition figures had either been killed or driven from the country and the opposition press silenced. They could cite Duarte's triumph at the polls as proof that the government was finally "democratic" and therefore worthy of U.S. support. Similarly, Vinicio Cerezo's civilian government in Guatemala makes U.S. aid much easier to secure. But the Guatemalan military knows that nothing has changed. A top Guatemalan army officer explained:

---

48. Howard Friel and Michelle Joffroy, "Media Manipulation in Costa Rica," *CovertAction,* no. 26, Summer 1986, 39.

49. IFDP Interview, San Jose, Costa Rica, Sept. 1984.

50. For a fuller discussion see Edward S. Herman and Frank Brodhead, *Demonstration Elections: U.S.-Staged Elections in the Dominican Republic, Vietnam, and El Salvador* (Boston: South End Press, 1984).

51. Miles, "The Real War," 36.

Vinicio [Cerezo] is a project of ours. . . . This civilian project is really a military project. We can defend the country better this way. That's why we were the first to press for elections, and that's why we want them to succeed.[52]

In Liberia, General Doe's election is used to justify U.S. support; never mind that he handpicked the parties allowed to run, and that all opposition parties denounced the election as a fraud.[53]

LOCAL FORCES DO THE JOB

Civic actions, yes. Propaganda, yes. Both are part of low intensity conflict. But we do not want to downplay its specifically military component. Here, too, the strategy is considerably more subtle than just "sending Marines ashore." Quick, surgical strikes by U.S. forces, like the 1983 U.S. invasion of Grenada, are one aspect, but not the primary motif of low-intensity-conflict strategy.

The Vietnam War debacle underlined for U.S. military planners that U.S. troops could actually be an obstacle to victory in the third world. To carry out U.S. strategic objectives, indigenous military forces must be better prepared. "That is one reason why we place so much emphasis upon military and police training and assistance programs," notes the State Department's Robert Oakley, chief of counterterrorism.[54] To George Shultz, El Salvador demonstrates how well this strategy can work:

---

52. Stephen Kinzer, "Walking the Tightrope in Guatemala," *The New York Times Magazine,* Nov. 9, 1986.

53. Ernest Harsch, "A Dictatorship Propped Up by Washington," *Intercontinental Press,* Apr. 21, 1986, 252.

54. Barry, *Low Intensity Conflict,* 29, quoting *Current Policy,* State Department, no. 744.

In El Salvador, we see how the wise provision of sufficient
economic and military assistance obviates the need to consider any direct involvement of American forces.[55]

Besides more loans and grants for arms, the consequence is
more U.S. military advisers assigned to the third world and
more third-world officers brought to U.S. military training
schools. Since 1950, the United States has already trained over
500,000 military personnel from eighty-five countries.[56] By
1986, in violation of the Neutrality Act, the United States was
training contras on American soil to overthrow the Nicaraguan government.[57]

Because in low intensity conflict the enemy is within a nation's borders, melding military and police operations is crucial. In helping this process along, the Reagan administration
faced an obstacle—a 1975 ban on U.S. aid to foreign police,
intelligence operations, and penal systems. The ban had been
Congress's response to public pressure after evidence surfaced
that some of the world's most brutal police forces—including
Iran's Savak and Idi Amin's "public safety unit"[58]—had been
trained under U.S. programs.[59] From its earliest days in office,
the Reagan administration pushed to end the ban,[60] and finally
succeeded in getting Congress to partially lift it after four

---

55. George Shultz, "Low-Intensity Warfare: The Challenge of Ambiguity," Department of State, *Current Policy,* no. 783, Jan. 1986, 4.

56. Edward S. Herman (Professor of Finance at the Wharton School of the University of Pennsylvania), "U.S. Sponsorship of State Terrorism," *CovertAction,* no. 26,
Summer 1986, 30.

57. "Contra's Training Near Eglin AFB, U.S. Officials Say," *Miami Herald,* Nov.
28, 1986.

58. Holly Burkhalter and Alita Paine, "Our Overseas Cops," *The Nation,* Sept. 14,
1985, 197.

59. The prohibition is Section 660 of the Foreign Assistance Act. Costa Rica
represents one exception to this rule. It should also be noted that neither CIA training
nor aid to train drug enforcement officials was outlawed under Section 660. (Interview with Caleb Rossiter from the Senate Arms Control and Foreign Policy Caucus,
July 1986.)

60. Burkhalter and Paine, "Our Overseas Cops," 197.

U.S. Marines were gunned down in San Salvador in 1985.[61]

To justify its military training, the State Department proudly notes that its graduates go on to hold positions of influence or prominence in their countries.[62] Two such influential and prominent graduates include Chile's General Pinochet and Nicaragua's former ruler Anastasio Somoza.[63] Despite this record, the training of foreign military and police continues to be sold on the rationale that it increases professionalism, including heightened respect for human rights.

Experience suggests otherwise. Forces trained during the 1960s as part of President Kennedy's Alliance for Progress included Somoza's National Guard whose brutality is legendary. After U.S. training, Guatemala's military-dominated governments led the hemisphere as violators of human rights, responsible for over 100,000 deaths since the mid-fifties.[64] One overview of the 1970s showed that twenty-six of the thirty-five governments using systematic torture were recipients of U.S. military or economic aid.[65] And any admonishment against the use of torture that might be taught in our training programs is now contradicted by U.S. actions. In 1983, for the first time, the U.S. government began licensing instruments of torture for international sale.[66]

---

61. Ibid. The Reagan administration has started providing assistance under the foreign aid bill. Section 711 allows assistance to law enforcement agents.

62. AID, *Congressional Presentation for Security Assistance Programs, FY 1987.* vol. 1, 65.

63. Samuel Fitch, "Human Rights and U.S. Military Aid Programs," *WOLA Report.* Washington Office on Latin America, Washington, D.C., July 1985, 3.

64. "Guatemala: A Human Rights Tragedy." For a recent overview of human rights in Guatemala, see: *Guatemala Revised: How the Reagan Administration Finds "Improvement" in Human Rights in Guatemala.* An Americas Watch Report, New York, Sept. 1985, 3. For more on Guatemala's record, see reports from Amnesty International, Americas Watch, and the Washington Office on Latin America.

65. Noam Chomsky and Edward S. Herman, *The Washington Connection and Third World Fascism* (Boston: South End Press, 1979), frontispiece and notes, 361.

66. Interview with Robert Mitchell, an international marketing consultant, June 1984. For more detail, see the U.S. Department of Commerce, Export Administration Regulations (1983 and before), supplement no. 1, sec. 5999B.

Little explicit discussion of human rights goes on in U.S. training courses, on the assumption that U.S. commitment to human rights is self-evident in other topics.[67] Trainees brought to the United States for instruction simply absorb humanitarian values, goes the theory. In 1986, when Phoenix, Arizona, businessman Saul Diskin learned that Salvadorans linked to the death squads were being trained by his own city's police, he responded:

> I keep asking why do people need training to refrain from murdering and raping nuns and *campesinos* and committing massacres. That's not something they are going to learn not to do by riding around in Phoenix police cars. . . . Training these people in computers and modern intelligence techniques will only make them more efficient killers.[68]

Newspaper pictures of tortured bodies, hands roped behind their backs, have come to signify the horror of Central America for many Americans. In these images most Americans see an uncivilized third-world military run amok. What they do *not* see is the mark of U.S. training, funded with their own tax dollars.

OUR SECRET SOLDIERS AND COUNTERTERROR

In addition to providing arms and upgrading third-world military and police forces, the U.S. military has identified a key role in low intensity conflict for what are called U.S. Special Forces—commando units trained in guerrilla warfare, terrorist actions, intelligence, as well as psychological operations. The Green Berets are perhaps the best-known example of counterinsurgency forces. Since 1981, the Reagan administra-

---

67. Fitch, "Human Rights and U.S. Military Aid Programs," 2.

68. Vince Bielski and Dennis Bernstein, "Inviting Death Squads to Tea," *In These Times*, Aug. 20–Sept. 2, 1986.

tion has quadrupled funds for these troops.[69] These secret soldiers of the Pentagon often operate like a uniformed CIA, working in every branch of the armed forces. Unlike the CIA, however, which must report its covert operations to Congress, the movement of Special Forces need not be approved by Congress.[70]

From the mid-sixties, counterterror has been integral to Special Forces operations. The CIA and the Green Berets helped set up paramilitary, counterterrorist groups in Guatemala to target dissidents, and similar groups were established in the 1970s in El Salvador. These paramilitary organizations became the notorious death squads that still plague Central America.[71]

Throughout this chapter, we have used the government's term "counterterror." But what *is* counterterror? Essentially, says Edward Herman of the University of Pennsylvania's Wharton School and an authority on terrorism, counterterror is a handy euphemism the U.S. government and its allies use to describe their own acts of terror. When in 1985, for example, the Reagan administration requested $5 million for the Guatemalan police and security forces—among the most brutal in Latin America—it was part of a counterterrorism package.[72]

U.S. counterterror acts began coming to light in the early 1980s. In 1983 a CIA manual—*Psychological Operations in Guerrilla Warfare*—surfaced in Central America, revealing that the CIA encourages killing of civilians in its war against the Nicaraguan government. The targeting of government teachers,

69. Barry, *Low Intensity Conflict,* 23. See also "America's Secret Soldiers: The Buildup of U.S. Special Operations Forces," *The Defense Monitor,* Center for Defense Information, vol. 14, no. 2, 1985.

70. IFDP telephone interview with Major Doug Coffey of the Secretary of the Army, Office of Public Affairs, Oct. 1986.

71. Allan Nairn, "Confessions of a Death Squad Officer," *The Progressive,* Mar. 1986.

72. Edward S. Herman, "Power and the Semantics of Terrorism," *CovertAction,* no. 26, Summer 1986, 9.

health, and agricultural workers for assassination is not *indiscriminate* violence, however, as some opponents claimed; it is part of a systematic policy of showing the Nicaraguan government's weakness and the opposition's strength. Low intensity conflict is terror to make a political point.

In 1984, President Reagan's directive endorsing preemptive strikes and reprisals against terrorists in other countries gave explicit presidential sanction to what had long been part of low intensity conflict's counterterror strategy.[73] The 1983 CIA-supported mining of Nicaraguan harbors and the blowing up of fuel storage tanks on the Nicaraguan coast are just two examples. The stated rationale is now broad enough to cover virtually any action against whomever Washington labels a terrorist.

AND ON THE HOME FRONT

But the "most pressing problem [for low intensity conflict] is not in the third world," laments former Rand Corporation president George Tanham. It is "here at home in the struggle for the minds of people."[74] The enemy to be fought here is the "Vietnam syndrome,"—Americans' reluctance to intervene abroad, arising from fear of losing American lives and undermining the U.S. economy in drawn-out, faraway wars.

Equally problematic is the Carter-era legacy of a foreign policy sensitive to human rights concerns. But perhaps most troubling to low-intensity-conflict strategists are Americans' democratic values. It is our "concern for or belief in the sacredness of life, individual autonomy, freedom of choice, and justice" that makes it so difficult to galvanize the national will

73. National Security Decision Directive 138, signed by President Reagan, Apr. 3, 1984. "U.S. Plans Tough Policy on Terrorism," *The New York Times.* Apr. 17, 1984, 3.

74. Barry, *Low Intensity Conflict.* 14, quoting Stephen T. Hosmer, *Constraints on U.S. Strategy in Third World Conflict* (Santa Monica: Air Force report prepared for the U.S. Air Force by the Rand Corporation, 1985).

behind low intensity conflict, worries military strategist Dr.
Sam Sarkesian, writing in a U.S. Air Force journal.[75]

To overcome these multiple obstacles, low-intensity-conflict
strategists are pursuing a number of clearly thought out tactics.

First, the value framework of the American people must be
altered so that they will accept support for nondemocratic
systems. Americans must be made to understand that to protect our way of life, we must do things that "may not be in
accord with . . . the American political system in morality and
ethics," says Sarkesian.[76] Surely the American people will be
more likely to condone such compromises if they can be made
to perceive all third-world insurgents as terrorists. In mid-
1985, *The New York Times* reported that the administration
deliberately began calling the Nicaraguan government and
the Salvadoran rebels terrorists to "bring any future military
strike or other action under the oratorical umbrella of the
Reagan Administration campaign against terrorists." A senior
government official told the *Times,* "We have every right to
strike back at terrorists. That's our stated policy."[77]

To enlist the support of the American people, the administration must also shape citizens' perceptions of the governments the United States supports. The Philippines under
Ferdinand Marcos is a good example. In the aftermath of
Marcos winning a rigged presidential election in 1981, Vice
President George Bush toasted him: "We stand with you, sir.
. . . We love your adherence to democratic principles and
democratic processes."[78] Today Washington repeatedly calls
the Central American countries—with the pointed exclusion

---

75. Dr. Sam Sarkesian, "Low Intensity Conflict: Concepts, Principles, and Policy
Guidelines," *Air University Review.* Jan.–Feb. 1985, 9.

76. Ibid., 9, 11.

77. Miles, "The Real War, 41. For a fuller discussion, see Edward S. Herman,
The Real Terror Network: Terrorism in Fact and Propaganda (Boston: South End Press,
1982).

78. Cited in Kwitny, *Endless Enemies.* 305, and in Bello et al., *Development Debacle*
(San Francisco: Food First Books, Institute for Food and Development Policy, Philippine Solidarity Network, 1982), 1–2.

of Nicaragua—democracies despite the fact that most of these democracies kill their opposition, abduct their troublesome civilians, control dissent, and block any substantive change to meet majority needs.

U.S. Security Assistance and Growing Insecurity

In pursuit of a foreign policy blinded by a false definition of our national interest, the United States is not only shoring up repressive governments but coaching them in a multifaceted strategy to fight the inevitable resistance they engender. The strategy is subtle, systematic, and far-reaching. But it cannot succeed. And it cannot serve our national interest.

Indeed, it is already a proven failure. In many ways, today's security strategy, specifically the development of low intensity conflict, is a repeat—writ large—of Alliance for Progress initiatives begun by President Kennedy in the early 1960s, in which billions of dollars in military and economic aid went to Latin American governments.[79] Were the poor majorities mollified? Armed resistance to the governments in Central America is greater now than then. Today's military dominated foreign aid policy cannot work because of several flaws in its logic.

First, low intensity conflict seeks to gain the loyalty of the people, in part, by gestures of concern for the health and welfare of the poor, while avoiding reforms involving the distribution of the society's productive resources. But, as more and more resources are poured into the local military establishment, such a heavy burden is placed on the government that it cannot even offer Band-Aids to its people.

Second, the concept of nation building—putting a respectable face on local governing institutions—assumes that local

---

79. For an excellent history of the Alliance for Progress in Central America, see Walter LaFeber, *Inevitable Revolutions: The United States in Central America* (New York: W. W. Norton, 1983).

elites feel at least some stake in making their country work. Experience gives us little reason to think that this assumption is realistic. Conservatively estimated, the monied elite of El Salvador has drained that country of more than a billion dollars since the late seventies.[80] How can nation building proceed if the only people with wealth invest it in Miami, not San Salvador? Even more to the point, the same elite groups that the Pentagon counts on to use our aid to stabilize their societies are simply stealing a good part of it to buy luxuries for themselves (like Mobutu's Belgian castle replete with a moat, or his 1982 state trip to Disney World with an entourage of eighty people!).[81]

Third, low-intensity-conflict theory hinges on the conviction that it can work because it can remain hidden from close scrutiny by the American people. It assumes that unless "our boys are coming home in body bags" Americans will keep their eyes shut. But, can low intensity conflict really avoid sending U.S. troops eventually? Having U.S. Green Berets and other special forces involved in military action alongside indigenous troops is "like carrying a loaded gun," says Air Force Lieutenant John T. Chain, and that gun operates on a hair-trigger.[82] Once U.S. soldiers are killed, pressure to launch full-scale intervention would mount. Once U.S. troops are involved overtly and at risk, the very basis of low intensity conflict—its low profile—would be lost.

Fourth, U.S. security strategies stumble on the age-old "ends and means" dilemma. Low-intensity-conflict theorist Sam Sarkesian flatly states: "low intensity conflicts do not conform to democratic notions. . . . Survival is the ultimate morality."[83] But, quite practically, *can* good ends be achieved by compromised means? The moral lesson we learn as children,

---

80. William Goodfellow, "U.S. Economic Aid to El Salvador: Where is the Money Going?" *International Policy Report* (Washington, D.C.: Center for International Policy, May 1984).

81. Kwitny, *Endless Enemies,* 86, 99–100.

82. Barry, *Low Intensity Conflict,* 24.

83. Sarkesian, "Low Intensity Conflict," 11.

becomes simple realism in adult life: ultimately, the methods used to reach a goal *do* end up determining the outcome. U.S. security assistance flouts this moral lesson. Justifying low intensity conflict as part of a crusade against Soviet totalitarianism, its theorists suggest that the United States can effectively use manipulation and deception to create open, democratic societies. They claim that terror can wipe out terror.

Fifth, and related to all of the above, current U.S. security assistance is built on a further contradiction—that a nation can attain stability and security by denying the majority of its people precisely these two essential human needs. U.S. security assistance programs pay not even lip service to the need to address the root of poverty, which is the grossly concentrated control over a nation's resources. But how can the majority ever achieve security if they are denied access to land or decently paying jobs?

The most glaring flaw in our current aid strategy is this: it assumes that people are dumb and spineless, and poor people especially so. It takes for granted that they can be bought off with Band-Aids and intimidated by the threat of death. It assumes that the church and other social workers will not see through the thin patina of humanitarian concern that low intensity conflict wears.

In fact, many poor people understand all too well the roots of their misery. They know democracy when they see it—and when they don't. "We haven't seen democracy," an elderly Salvadoran refugee told an American journalist in 1986, "not even half a fingernail of democracy. We receive only bombs."[84] Nor do low-intensity-conflict theorists understand that suffering can make people fearless. Describing the Salvadoran mothers whose children have been killed by government forces, the same journalist observed, "These women remain formidable because they have faced the unimaginable,

---

84. Renny Golden, "El Salvador's Refugees: Targets in a New Style War," *Christianity and Crisis,* Sept. 8, 1986, 293.

the death or disappearance of a child, and they are no longer afraid."[85]

Many poor people also see through the military's claims that it is acting to protect them. "They say they are looking out for our national security. What national security?" a Honduran peasant woman asked one of our staff.

> We Hondurans are dying of hunger, we're not interested in fighting our neighbors. The national security they are protecting is that of their own big stomachs. They're protecting the fat checks that come pouring in from the United States.[86]

Throughout this chapter, we have shown that an increasingly militarized U.S. foreign aid program protects the security of the privileged. Such a policy not only violates the principles our nation espouses but it ultimately defeats *our own interests as well.*

Allocating our aid dollars according to a narrow definition of our national interest—whoever is not actively allied to the Soviet Union is automatically a friend of the United States—ultimately backfires. Rooted in fear, such an aid policy is blind to the social realities within countries whose governments the United States supports. Unable to acknowledge the legitimate demands of the desperately poor majorities in many of these countries, U.S. policymakers contribute to precisely the global *in*stability they claim to loathe.

In the next two chapters we turn to those aspects of foreign aid which many U.S. citizens want to think of as America at its best—development assistance and food aid. Is their role more in keeping with the values of most Americans and with our national interest?

---

85. Ibid., 293.

86. IFDP Interview with Elvia Alvarado, July 1986. See Elvia Alvarado, edited by Medea Benjamin, *Don't Be Afraid, Gringo: A Honduran Woman Speaks from the Heart* (San Francisco: Food First Books, 1987).

Three

Development
Assistance —
For Whose Development?

"DEVELOPMENT ASSISTANCE"—funding for rural roads
or farm credit schemes—is probably closer to what most of us
think of as foreign aid than either the Economic Support Fund
or military aid. But development assistance is actually a small
part of our foreign aid program—only eighteen percent (recall Chart 1).

Development assistance initiatives include education and
health intervention, such as life-saving therapy for malnourished infants. But of all AID's programs, agriculture and rural
development is claimed to be the one most directly attacking
the root of people's poverty, and is by far the largest category
of development assistance.[1]

Here we ask: have AID's agriculture and rural development
projects proven helpful to the rural poor? And can they? To

---

1. In fiscal year 1986, agriculture made up forty-seven percent of the (proposed)
development assistance program. Population planning, fifteen percent; health, nine
percent; education, eleven percent; and "other," thirteen percent. The remaining five
percent went to the Sahel Development Program, which also includes a number of
agriculture and rural development projects. (U.S. Agency for International Development, *Congressional Presentation. Fiscal Year 1986.* main vol., 8.)

begin answering these questions requires a little history. The story begins a few years after the end of World War II.

THE EARLY YEARS

In the late 1940s, about the same time that the Marshall Plan was getting off the ground in Europe, the U.S. government was becoming increasingly worried about the political future of underdeveloped nations.[2] Policymakers feared that desperation born of extreme poverty, economic underdevelopment, and lack of political participation could cause the poor majorities in the third world to see communism as an attractive path to development. Economic growth for the third world was therefore seen as essential to countering the communist threat.[3]

To help stimulate that growth, Congress passed the Act for International Development in 1950, the antecedent to our present Development Assistance program. The act authorized money and technical assistance for poor countries. Once these poor nations received investment capital and western technology, it was believed, they would be launched onto a path of self-sustaining economic growth.

Throughout the 1960s, the development establishment did not question the wisdom of this model—or the appropriateness of western technology.[4] Aid was channeled into large-scale infrastructure like roads, hospitals, and hydroelectric dams, and to importing the U.S. technology needed to carry

---

2. The Marshall Plan was the precursor of the U.S. foreign assistance program. At a cost to American taxpayers of $60 billion (in today's dollars), the Marshall Plan sought to rebuild the strength and power of Europe's business classes after World War II.

3. This section draws heavily on Elliott and Victoria Morss, *U.S. Foreign Aid: An Assessment of New and Traditional Development Strategies* (Boulder, Col.: Westview Press, 1982), chapter 2. See also by the same authors: *The Future of Western Development Assistance* (Boulder, Col.: Westview Press, 1986).

4. We refer here to AID, the World Bank, and other regional development banks, and to the many economists, political scientists, and other academics who advised these aid institutions.

out these projects. Most investments flowed into the cities, reflecting our own economy's bias and the weight of political power in recipient countries.

Although the question of who would benefit from the over-all growth was not entirely ignored, policymakers didn't fret too much about the poor. Third-world economies were assumed to be just like ours—only in an earlier stage of development. W. W. Rostow's *The Stages of Economic Growth* became the development gospel.[5] According to Rostow, all economies would automatically industrialize and thus "develop," once certain preconditions were met. As national output expanded, all classes of society would be lifted up to enjoy a higher

CHART 7: TOP TEN RECIPIENTS OF U.S. DEVELOPMENT ASSISTANCE 1981–1986
($ millions)

Country	Development Assistance $
*1. India	$539.5
*2. Bangladesh	470.4
3. Indonesia	401.8
4. El Salvador	337.7
*5. Sri Lanka	224.7
6. Honduras	206.6
7. Philippines	194.1
8. Peru	166.7
*9. Sudan	153.8
10. Yemen	148.6

*Countries designated low income by The World Bank, *World Development Report 1985*

Source: U.S. Agency For International Development, *Congressional Presentations. Fiscal Years 1983–1987.*

---

5. W. W. Rostow, *The Stages of Economic Growth* (Cambridge, Mass.: Cambridge University Press, 1960). See also "The Take-Off Into Self-sustained Economic Growth," *Economic Journal.* 66, Mar. 1956, 25–48.

standard of living. Since the theory acknowledged that growth incentives would have to go to those at the top of the economic ladder, only indirectly benefiting those at the bottom, it became known as the "trickle-down theory."

Although many third-world countries grew rapidly during the fifties and sixties, it's not clear how much foreign aid contributed to their growth. While some studies have found a positive link between aid and growth, as the theory predicted, others discovered just the opposite relationship.[6]

While the effect of aid on economic growth might be open to debate, one outcome was hard to miss: poverty was not being eradicated. Some scholars argued that economic growth was actually accompanied by a worsening of the income distribution in the short run, causing poverty to deepen.[7] In 1973, a widely debated study of seventy-four developing countries by economists Irma Adelman and Cynthia Morris concluded that the trickle-down theory was a fraud:

> There is no automatic, or even likely, trickling down of the benefits of economic growth to the poorest segments of the population in low-income countries. On the contrary, the absolute position of the poor tends to deteriorate as a consequence of economic growth.[8]

Others showed that it was impractical: the rates of growth necessary even to create the potential for alleviating poverty—

---

6. For a review, see Robert Cassen and Associates, *Does Aid Work?* (Oxford, U.K.: Oxford University Press, 1986), chapter 2.

7. This argument was originally made by Stanley Kuznets, an economist at Harvard University. (See S. Kuznets, "Economic Growth and Income Inequality," *American Economic Review*, 45, no. 2, Mar. 1955, 1–28). Also, for a comprehensive review of the literature on this subject, see Arne Bigsten, *Income Distribution and Development: Theory, Evidence and Policy* (London: Heinemann Educational Books, 1983), chapter 5. How long a period "the short run" is remains open to question, of course. One study cited by Bigsten estimated that a century would have to pass before the income distribution in many countries would begin to improve again! Ibid., 66.

8. Irma Adelman and Cynthia Taft Morris, *Economic Growth and Social Equity in Developing Countries* (Stanford, Calif.: Stanford University Press, 1973), 189.

nine to eleven percent per year—were completely out of reach.[9] And even if economic growth could theoretically ease poverty over the long term, many asked whether it was conscionable to wait—while people suffered—if direct economic intervention could help now. Economist Amartya Sen estimated that it would have taken Sri Lanka somewhere between 58 and 152 years of economic growth to attain the same high level of life expectancy it achieved through concerted public action on behalf of the poor.[10]

A"NEW DIRECTION"?

In response to widespread disillusionment with trickle-down, Congress was pushed in the early 1970s to take a number of steps to redefine U.S. development aid.

The Foreign Assistance Act of 1973 was the first attempt to ensure that development aid would directly attack poverty. This New Directions legislation, as it came to be known, called for aid projects "which most directly benefit the poorest majority of the people in these countries and which enable them to participate more effectively in the development process."[11] To deal more directly with the problems of the poor, the bill defined new categories of assistance in areas such as

---

9. See, for instance, Keith Griffin and Jeffrey James, *The Transition to Egalitarian Development: Economic Policies for Structural Change in the Third World* (New York: St. Martin's Press, 1981), chapter 1. Griffin was part of an International Labour Organization (ILO) team that estimated the growth rates which would be necessary to meet the basic needs of the poorest 20 percent of the population within one generation, assuming no redistributive policies. The ILO estimates suggest that Asia (excluding China) would require an *annual* growth rate of 9.7 percent to meet basic human needs by the year 2000; China would need a growth rate of 6 percent per annum; Africa, 11.1 percent; Latin America, between 8.7 and 9.4 percent; and the Middle East, 11.3 percent. Such rates are, needless to say, considerably above the actual rates of growth experienced by these regions over the last several decades.

10. Amartya Sen, "Economic Development: Some Strategic Issues," in Altaf Gauhar, ed. *The Rich and the Poor: Development, Negotiations, and Cooperation—An Assessment* (London: Third World Foundation for Social and Economic Studies, 1983), 47.

11. Mutual Development and Cooperation Act of 1973, *Report of the Committee on Foreign Affairs on H. R. 9390* (Washington, D.C., U.S. Government Printing Office, July 20, 1973), 1.

agriculture and rural development, health, nutrition, and population planning.

Shortly thereafter, famine hit both Asia and Africa, food prices soared, and "world hunger" hit the international marquee. Citizen groups and development specialists pushed to extend the New Directions mandate, and succeeded with the passage of the 1975 International Development and Food Assistance Act. It stressed "basic human needs," "appropriate technology," and "participation"—the buzzwords of the new "bottom up" development philosophy.

In the seventies new faces began to appear within the U.S. aid institutions. Young people, disillusioned with U.S. foreign policy and the misuse of aid during the Vietnam War, were taking jobs with AID—the government agency charged with overseeing U.S. Development Assistance funds—with the express intention of improving our aid program. Among this group were former Peace Corps volunteers who had seen firsthand the havoc many of our foreign aid policies had wrought.

"BASIC NEEDS": COULD IT WORK?

While within AID some serious soul-searching was underway, outside the agency many Americans were beginning to question whether U.S. aid was actually helping the poor abroad. In 1975, our educational center—the Institute for Food and Development Policy (IFDP)—was just getting off the ground. Our first book *Food First: Beyond the Myth of Scarcity,* which questions the impact of official U.S. foreign aid, joined many other voices. In Boston, Oxfam-America was beginning to look for alternative approaches to development aid. In Washington, groundwork was underway for the Development Group for Alternative Policies, whose later studies of aid we use here and in chapter 4. Church organizations were collaborating to launch the Interreligious Taskforce on U.S. Food

Policy to influence congressional votes related to domestic and world hunger.

In 1980, we published our first book focused entirely on the impact of U.S. foreign aid—*Aid as Obstacle.* It questioned whether the "basic needs" aid strategy was really any better than the earlier trickle-down. Our research in the third world,[12] interviews with aid officials and peasants, and our reading of endless aid project evaluations (many sponsored by AID itself) convinced us that the project assistance given during the 1970s did not—in fact, could not—significantly improve conditions for the world's poor majority. Even though U.S. development aid was supposedly targeting the poor, it seldom reached them. In 1985 a major report released by the World Bank and the International Monetary Fund (IMF) partially confirmed our findings. It acknowledged that the rural development programs of the 1970s "have usually been unable to benefit the 'poorest of the poor,' i.e., the lowest 20 percent or so of the rural income distribution."[13]

MAKING THE SMALL FARMER MORE PRODUCTIVE

In the logic of New Directions, a key strategy for overcoming hunger was making the small farmer more productive. More farm credit was supposed to do the trick. Few stopped to ask how credit would help the neediest group of all—those with no land. By the mid-seventies, the landless accounted for half or more of all rural people in at least twenty third-world countries.[14]

---

12. Often focusing on those very projects that AID and the World Bank said were most successful.

13. See Joint Ministerial Committee of the Board of Governors of the World Bank and the International Monetary Fund (Development Committee), "Aid for Development: The Key Issues—Supporting Materials for the Report of the Task Force on Concessional Flows," (Washington, D.C.: Development Committee, 1985), 41.

14. Milton J. Esman, *Landlessness and Near Landlessness in Developing Countries* (Ithaca, N.Y.: Cornell University, Center for International Studies, 1978).

Even many with land didn't have enough collateral—property or other assets—to qualify for the loans. One evaluation of twelve years of AID experience with small farmer credit programs concluded:

> The distribution of [subsidized interest rates] is highly skewed against the small farmer and the landless poor. . . . Existing agricultural credit agencies tend to channel the majority of lending to medium- and large-scale farmers.[15]

When small farmers *did* receive loans and increased their yields, their incomes did not necessarily climb. If production costs rose as fast (or faster) than yields, or prices for their crops fell because of greater supplies on the market, the farmers became poorer than ever.

FOREIGN AID AND "THE NET"

Foreign assistance can actually make the lives of the poor harder if it strengthens the forces opposed to their interests.

Consider a small village in Bangladesh that receives a deep tube well as part of an aid project. (A tube well is a mechanically drilled well in which water is lifted with a pump, usually for irrigation.) Although project planners report that the well provides water to an irrigation cooperative of twenty-five to fifty small farmers, in reality it is quickly usurped by the village's richest landlord who then charges others for using it. His new irrigation-generated wealth means that the landowner is in an even better position to push his indebted neighbors from the land.[16]

---

15. Joseph Lieberson, "A Synthesis of AID Experience: Small-Farmer Credit, 1973–1985," AID Evaluation Special Study, no. 41 (Washington, D.C.: AID, Oct. 1985), 11.

16. For a fuller discussion, see: Frances Moore Lappé, Joseph Collins, and David Kinley, *Aid As Obstacle* (San Francisco: Food First Books, 1980), chap. 7.

In the same vein, nothing seems more innocuous and generally beneficial than AID's program to build rural roads. Lack of rural roads, however, is hardly a crucial problem for poor subsistence farmers with little surplus to sell. The primary beneficiaries of the new roads are the more prosperous growers, especially those with enough surplus to sell in urban or export markets. As this small group of farmers is enriched, they are better able to buy up the land of their less well-off neighbors.

Even the best of New Directions development assistance failed to grasp these real obstacles to development. It assumed that the communities receiving the new resources were composed of people with common interests. In reality, they are communities at war. The minority who controls most of the assets uses its considerable power to ensure that any outside resources entering the village will accrue to it.

Perhaps no clearer picture of this reality has been drawn than that by the Bangladesh Rural Advancement Committee (BRAC), a development organization founded and controlled by Bangladeshis. After five months of intensive field work, relying on information mostly from poor, landless people, in 1980 BRAC produced a remarkable study: *The Net: Power Structure in Ten Villages*. And to what does the "net" refer? Development specialist Robert Chambers explains:

> Local elites stand as nets between the poorer people and the outside world, in the sense that they catch and trap resources and benefits.
>
> It is not just that the powerful intercept; it is also that the price [often a bribe] demanded for passing on benefits can exclude many of the poor. . . . Nor does this exclusion apply only to loans. We have . . . seen treatment for a broken leg withheld because the sum illegally demanded could not be raised.[17]

---

17. Robert Chambers, *Rural Development: Putting the Last First* (New York: Longman, 1983), 131–132.

The net surrounding the poor is often tightly woven. The "police, government officials and the larger landowners and traders have common interests and understandings," Chambers points out. They are thus "well placed to use deception, blackmail and violence to rob the poor."[18] And the poor have no recourse to justice. They do not know the law and cannot afford legal help. If they resist the demands of the rich, Chambers explains, the poor can be "brought to heel by a visit from the police, a threat of prosecution or arrest, the calling in of a debt, a refusal of employment, or violence."[19]

In studying New Directions aid, we learned this rule that expresses the fundamental contradiction within U.S. development assistance: *it's impossible to go through the power*ful *to reach the power*less.

THE REAGAN ERA

The failure of even New Directions U.S. aid to bring about development was easy to document, providing the Reagan administration a perfect opportunity to push its own agenda. From 1981 onward, economic growth was reinstated as the central goal of U.S. development assistance. Four years later, AID published its first long-term strategic plan, *Blueprint for Development.* It states that:

> Broad-based economic growth with increased employment and higher agricultural production will provide the income for better meeting basic human needs.[20]

In the Reagan administration's plan for the third world, the "engine of economic growth" is the private sector. Funneling aid directly to private business interests, claims AID, will gen-

---

18. Ibid., 133.

19. Ibid.

20. AID, *A Blueprint for Development: The Strategic Plan of the Agency for International Development* (Washington, D.C.: AID, 1985), iii.

erate new job opportunities and therefore improve living standards for the poor.[21]

In Guatemala, for example, $8 million in development assistance is going to provide loans and technical assistance for development of small and medium-sized businesses. According to the agency, beneficiaries will include about 150 small businessmen and 1,000 employees.[22] How does AID define a small businessman? Anyone with up to $250,000 in net fixed assets. (Medium businesses are defined as those with up to $2 million in assets.) By this definition, only the biggest Guatemalan businesses would fail to qualify!

In Kenya, $36 million is going to a private enterprise project aimed at export-oriented agricultural businesses. Another upcoming project will direct $40 million to a scheme that will help in providing technology and improving marketing for businesses.[23]

In Dominica, AID is helping the Banana Industry Rehabilitation Project to reorganize Dominica's banana industry along private lines.[24] The aid agreement stipulates that all farm supplies must be purchased from U.S. firms and sold to farmers at prevailing market prices—no longer duty-free and subsidized, as they had been in the past. The use of private U.S. consultants as industry advisers is also built into the plan. Moreover, the only herbicide being made available under the program is paraquat, a chemical suspected of damaging the human respiratory system and fetus, and which has been

---

21. See "Private Enterprise: The Key To Development," *AID Highlights*, vol. 1, no. 2, Summer 1984, 1.

22. AID, *Congressional Presentation, FY 1987*, annex III, Latin America and the Caribbean, 128.

23. *Trends in Foreign Aid, 1977–86*, study prepared by the Foreign Affairs and National Defense Division, Congressional Research Service for the Select Committee on Hunger, U.S. House of Representatives, Nov. 1986, 17.

24. AID *Congressional Presentation, FY 1986*, annex III, Latin America and the Caribbean, 117. This $1.7 million appears to be funded technically by ESF, though it's described under "development activities" and there may be some counterpart funding.

banned in the United States for the last ten years.[25] For poor farmers, the results of the banana industry's reorganization have meant setbacks—higher production costs and lower prices for their crops, according to the Washington-based Development Group for Alternative Policies. Administrative costs have also climbed.[26]

A Lack of Technology?

True to its philosophy of the last two decades, AID still cites low productivity—particularly in agriculture—as a primary cause of hunger in the third world.[27] If poor farmers were producing more, the agency argues, they would be better able to feed themselves and their families. Similarly, the low productivity of workers in such countries is a "fundamental cause of low earnings."[28] (AID's analysis fails to explain why third-world workers in hi-tech manufacturing are not lifted out of poverty, in spite of their impressive productivity.)

In agriculture, where productivity measured by output per hour or worker is often quite low, AID's solution is new technology.[29] It will therefore research, develop, and transfer new technologies to third-world settings. These needn't be expensive or complex; in fact, they should be inexpensive, commercially viable, and appropriate to the local setting, says AID.[30]

---

25. Atherton Martin, Steve Hellinger, and David Solomon, *Prospects and Reality: The CBI Revisited* (Washington, D.C.: The Development Group for Alternative Policies, Inc., Nov. 1985), 32.

26. Ibid., 10, 34.

27. *Blueprint for Development.* 30.

28. Ibid., 25, 31.

29. Output *per acre* is often impressive. Small farmers in the third world typically produce two or more times greater output per acre than the largest growers.

30. See, for example, *Blueprint for Development.* 22, or *Facts About AID.* a one-page fact sheet published by the Agency for International Development (no date).

This would be all well and good, *if* lack of technology were the limiting factor. But for most of the world's poor, it is not lack of technology which gives rise to hunger. Rather, the poor lack land and the money to buy the tools and other farm inputs they need. Nearly a billion rural people are without land in the third world the United Nations estimates.[31] Even in Africa, where absolute landlessness is often not the problem, many of the poorest farmers have been pushed onto plots that are too small and infertile to support them.[32]

Among the poor who have land and reap low yields, the problem is often not that the technology doesn't exist but that they cannot afford it. Zimbabwe's small farmers could increase yields only after the government raised producer prices and shifted credit and agricultural assistance to meet their needs. The breakthrough resulted from a *policy change,* not a technological advance.[33]

In sum, it's not the lack of technology—appropriate or otherwise—that is the real cause of poverty. The lack of access to land, credit, and fair marketing channels is the prior constraint. And these deficiencies are themselves symptoms of people's powerlessness. Without addressing this underlying cause of hunger, new technology cannot relieve it.

RISK AND RICHES

Above we described the "net" through which outside resources—including any new technology—must pass, and, how the rich are able to intercept the benefits, strengthening their position at the expense of the poor. The capacity to handle risk

---

31. "Rural Poverty," paper prepared by the U.N. Food and Agriculture Organization for World Food Day, 1986, 2.

32. See, for example: Stephen K. Commins, Michael F. Lofchie, and Rhys Payne, eds., *Africa's Agrarian Crisis* (Boulder, Col.: Lynne Rienner, 1986).

33. Carole Collins and Steve Askin, "Zimbabwe's Agricultural Gains Set Pace for Region," *National Catholic Reporter,* Aug. 2, 1985. For background: Paula Park and Tony Jackson, *Lands of Plenty, Lands of Scarcity: Agricultural Policy and Peasant Farmers in Zimbabwe and Tanzania* (Oxford, U.K.: Oxfam, 1985).

plays a critical part in this process, which apparently AID does not grasp.

In the agency's approach to agricultural "research and extension" (the spreading of information about new farming techniques), a small group of "progressive" farmers—those considered to be leaders and innovators—are identified to receive the new technology. It is assumed that their success using it will inspire the rest of the community to follow suit.

But most technologies being developed and promoted by AID are not for low-resource food producers "who generally seek to minimize risk rather than maximize production," notes a study by the U.S. Office of Technology Assessment (OTA).[34] The problem is that the usual package of farm supplies is too expensive for poor farmers.[35] "Consequently," concludes the report, "frustrated [government] agents work mostly with the more 'progressive' farmers who have the financial means to purchase the packages, and the majority of low-resource producers are excluded."[36] This progressive farmer approach to agricultural assistance was widely discredited in the 1970s.

Thus, it's not surprising that of all AID's development efforts, agriculture has had the worst record of technology transfer. This was the conclusion of a major 1984 report commissioned by the agency—based on 308 project evaluations and audit reports. The reason, its authors noted, was not that technology wasn't available, but that, after deliberate and careful consideration, farmers had decided not to take the risk.[37] In Kenya, for example, large farmers successfully

---

34. The study focuses on AID's approach to technology transfer, specifically in Africa. U.S. Office of Technology Assessment, "Africa Tomorrow: Issues in Technology, Agriculture, and U.S. Foreign Aid" (Washington, D.C.: OTA, Dec. 1984), 27.

35. Ibid., 51.

36. Ibid.

37. See Development Associates, Inc. "Lessons Learned From AID Program Experience in FY 1984: A Review of the Year's Project Evaluation and Audit Reports, World-wide," draft report prepared for AID, Aug. 3, 1985. Other AID project evaluations have reached similar conclusions. "These technologies, by their very

adopted an AID-introduced hybrid variety of maize, but the smallest farmers were afraid to try it out because they couldn't afford the risk of a crop failure. The project helped widen the income gap between large and small farmers.[38]

APPROPRIATE TECHNOLOGY: AID'S BIND

In its 1975 foreign aid legislation, Congress authorized AID to promote "capital saving technology" (CST), or technology which relies more on labor (which the third world has in abundance) than on capital (which is scarce).[39] Yet, in a 1984 review of the legislation's implementation, the General Accounting Office found that many AID missions they visited weren't even aware that Washington was still endorsing this policy.[40] This is not too surprising given that barely a tenth of the 1984 development assistance budget goes to CST projects.[41]

One constraint on AID attempts at transferring appropriate technology is that part of its mandate is to generate business for U.S. corporations. In fact, AID boasts that seventy percent of foreign aid expenditures return to purchase U.S. goods and services.[42] But U.S. corporations are less interested in selling "low-tech" items than bigger, fancier equipment on which more profits can be made.

---

nature, may be practical only for the better-off households," according to: AID Program Evaluation Report, no. 10, "Strengthening the Agricultural Research Capacity of the Less Developed Countries: Lessons from AID Experience," 28.

38. Ibid., 29.

39. AID has defined capital saving technology as technology which requires little capital per worker; is efficient on a small scale and widely replicable; is easily serviced and maintained while not requiring much education or training to operate; and involves the local community and uses locally available resources. (See U.S. Government Accounting Office, "Use of a Capital Saving Technology Approach in AID's Development Assistance Program," report no. NSIAD-84-142 (Washington, D.C.: U.S. GAO, July 26, 1984), i.

40. Ibid., 11.

41. Ibid., 4.

42. "Private Enterprise: The Key to Development," *AID Highlights*, vol. 1, no. 2, Summer 1984, 4.

Moreover, AID's need to export a model of agriculture that uses what American corporations have to sell is undoubtedly part of the reason it appears so oblivious to the widespread rethinking of the high-energy, monocultural model, known as the Green Revolution.[43] Even where the new seeds, fertilizer, pesticides, and irrigation associated with the Green Revolution have brought forth the greatest increases in production— in Southeast Asia—hunger is still widespread, if not worse than before. Can AID be unaware that when third-world farmers are locked into petrochemical-dependent agriculture, they find their profits squeezed by rising costs, just like American farmers?[44]

HAITI'S NEW PIGS

Nothing better illustrates AID's limited grasp of third-world reality, and the inherent constraints on its transfer of appropriate technology, than its response when Haiti's pig population contracted African swine fever.

For most rural Haitian households, pigs have long been a key to economic survival. A piglet could be bought for ten dollars, raised at little expense, and sold fifteen months later for as much as $180.[45] When emergencies and special occasions called for ready cash, having a pig to sell saved peasants from having to turn to unscrupulous loan sharks. Haiti's approximately one million home-grown pigs—adapted over many generations to local conditions—had many additional virtues. A 1986 study by Josh DeWind and David Kinley

---

43. See, for instance, AID's *Blueprint for Development.* 21. Reading this document, one would think that the Asian Green Revolution had ended hunger there, and now all that is needed is priority attention to developing high yielding grains for Africa— to make for an African Green Revolution.

44. For an introduction to the debate about the Green Revolution, see Myth Five in Frances Moore Lappé and Joseph Collins, *World Hunger: Twelve Myths* (San Francisco and New York: Food First Books/Grove Press, 1986).

45. Josh DeWind and David Kinley, *Aiding Migration: The Impact of International Development Assistance on Haiti.* Immigration Research Program, Center for the Social Sciences, Columbia University, 1986, 117.

published by Columbia University's Center for the Social Sciences, notes:

> Raised on human waste and farm by-products inedible by humans, pigs also provided a major source of sanitary control in rural areas and pig excrement provided a nitrogen-rich fertilizer for coffee, plantains, and other crops. Furthermore, the pigs' rooting in harvested fields helped to prepare soils for renewed cultivation and to eradicate insect pests such as the May Beetle larva.[46]

Thus, when African swine fever hit Haiti in 1978, already hard-pressed Haitians faced economic disaster. The disease itself killed about one-third of the pig population. Another third were slaughtered as local officials forced peasants to get rid of their pigs.

Then, with the help of the Organization of American States—with most of the funding coming from the United States—the Haitian government launched a campaign to eradicate Haiti's *entire* remaining pig population. U.S. support reflected fears that swine fever might harm the U.S. pork industry.

In theory, Haitians were to be compensated for their losses, but researchers in Haiti told us that few actually were.[47] One Haitian peasant complained bitterly that his compensation for a pig killed in the eradication campaign was a single cigarette!

AID played a critical role in the pig repopulation program. It set up two breeding centers to import Iowa pigs, strains utterly maladapted to Haitian conditions. The Iowa pigs require hygienic conditions, including cement corrals and frequent showers for relief from the heat. While Haitian pigs could eat anything and survive for long periods by foraging, Iowa pigs need high-protein, imported feed. The imported

---

46. Ibid., 118.

47. IFDP interviews with Groupe de Recherches Pour la Développement, Nov. 1986.

pigs, in other words, require better conditions than most Haitians can provide for *themselves.* (No wonder the Haitians call them "cochons bourgeois.") Surely, few can afford the new breed. Yet apparently no thought had been given to saving the well-adapted local pigs by quarantining uninfected ones for later breeding and repopulating.[48]

That eradicating Haiti's pigs would create a lucrative market for poultry in Haiti was not lost on the World Bank's International Finance Corporation (IFC). IFC made its first loan in Haiti to a corporation partially owned by the president of Haiti's Kentucky Fried Chicken chain. Rather than developing a program of chicken production benefiting peasants, the loan is for large-scale industrial poultry production in Port-au-Prince, which is expected to become a major supplier to Kentucky Fried Chicken. According to DeWind and Kinley, "the promotion of agro-industrial poultry production has effectively blocked small farmers from being able to replace their lost income by producing poultry."[49]

AID's involvement in the Haitian pig debacle reveals both its insensitivity to the needs of the Haitian poor and its arrogance in imposing solutions which better serve foreign interests. We were little surprised when a Haitian peasant told us his view of U.S. motivations: "The United States wanted to create a bigger market for their hogs and their feed exports. So they wiped out our pigs."

"Non-traditional" Exports: Dollars or Disaster?

Dovetailing perfectly with AID's notion of increasing the productivity of the poor is its program to push small, third-world farmers to give up basic food crops—or typical export crops

---

48. DeWind and Kinley, *Aiding Migration.*

49. Ibid., 125.

like coffee and cocoa—in favor of non-traditional export crops. For these schemes, AID is targeting peasants in Latin America and, increasingly, in Africa.

In AID's terminology, those crops colonialism promoted for export are "traditional"; all else is "non-traditional." (Never mind all the traditional crops that people cultivated for millennia before colonialism.) Everything from winter vegetables (like broccoli and snow peas) to herbs, spices, and even ornamental plants are being encouraged. U.S. consumers are seen as the primary market, although it's planned that some of the output will find its way to Western Europe as well. Diversifying into non-traditional exports will generate much needed foreign exchange, according to AID. Farmers, too, will benefit since the new crops bring higher prices than the food crops they had been cultivating. All of this sounds terrific, but are small farmers *really* likely to profit by shifting to specialty export crops?

THE CAULIFLOWER-BROCCOLI BUNGLE

Such projects are not new—at least one similar project that AID funded in Guatemala in the late seventies has now been thoroughly evaluated. What does it reveal about the claims for its successors?

Upon starting up operations in Guatemala, Alimentos Congelados Monte Bello, S.A. (ALCOSA), a wholly-owned subsidiary of the U.S. company Hanover Brands, set out to contract with small producers to grow broccoli, cauliflower, brussels sprouts, snow peas, and okra. The company planned to freeze and export the produce to the United States.[50] In exchange for the exclusive right to buy their harvests, AL-

---

50. ALCOSA received its AID funding through an intermediary, the Latin American Agribusiness Development Corporation (LAAD). For more detail, see Ken Kusterer, María Regina Estrada de Batres, and Jorge Xuya Cuxil, "The Social Impact of Agribusiness: A Case Study of ALCOSA in Guatemala," *AID Evaluation Special Study*. no. 4 (Washington, D.C.: U.S. AID, July 1981), 12.

COSA would provide farmers with credit, advice, and an assured price.

Guatemalan peasants were thus persuaded to take their fields out of corn and other locally consumed crops and put them into cauliflower and broccoli. For the first few years, farm incomes reportedly did improve. Some of the more enterprising even bought the crops of their neighbors to sell to ALCOSA at a slight profit. But their very success was creating a crisis.

At the direction of the company, ALCOSA's agronomists became increasingly aggressive in recruiting broccoli growers. Company agronomists seriously underestimated their potential, and these small, first-time growers began producing *double* the projected volume.

ALCOSA found itself swimming in broccoli. Every day, farmers delivered twice as much produce as the plant could handle. In response to this influx of broccoli, management temporarily suspended all purchases of cauliflower, the less profitable of the two crops. Handily for ALCOSA, its contracts with farmers only contained a one-way obligation: while farmers were required to sell their entire harvest to ALCOSA, ALCOSA was not obligated to buy what they produced.[51]

Cauliflower growers were desperate. With ALCOSA no longer willing to buy their produce, many turned to the local market, which rapidly became flooded with the unwanted vegetable. Prices plummeted. Among the hardest hit by the suspensions were farmers in the village of Chimachoy, who lost an average of $177—a good part of a year's income for most.

Although months later ALCOSA reinstated cauliflower purchases, many farmers still faced big problems. While prices for top-grade cauliflower had risen, they were not rising fast enough to offset the higher quality standards now being imposed by the company, and prices paid for second-grade cauli-

---

51. See Kusterer et al., "The Social Impact," 20.

flower hadn't risen at all since 1978. Moreover, new limitations were set on the amount of second-grade cauliflower ALCOSA would buy, leaving farmers without a steady or secure market for the growing volume of produce rejected as poor quality.[52]

The ALCOSA experience provides a sad lesson in what can happen when farmers with barely enough land to feed their families are encouraged to bet their survival on the vagaries of the international market. Even relatively well-off U.S. farmers are being destroyed by its unpredictability. Certainly, poor third-world farmers with no bargaining power cannot be expected to win.

Actually, ALCOSA may be one of the more successful projects of this type, since it theoretically provided a built-in market for farmers. In many of the agro-export projects AID is funding today, the problem of marketing remains completely unaddressed. In Honduras, for example, AID has spent about $10 million on a cashew growing and processing project. As in Guatemala, Honduran farmers were encouraged to take their land out of corn and plant it in the new crop. (We learned on a research trip to Honduras in 1986 that many peasants had actually been coerced into taking up cashews. If they didn't go along, they were threatened with having their rights to the land investigated by the Agrarian Reform Institute).[53]

When the cashews were finally ready to harvest, there was no workable marketing plan. The peasants had been promised $40 per one hundred pounds. But, in order to make the

---

52. To add insult to injury, some farmers were defrauded by company employees. In one exposed scheme, two farmers employed by ALCOSA were skimming a share of the other farmers' deliveries, netting them $100 a week in an area where the average wage was $2 a day. In another incident, ALCOSA's chief agronomist was accused of telling farmers to buy more inputs than they needed, so he could increase his illegal kickbacks from the suppliers. As a result, farmers' fertilizer costs were fifty percent higher than they should have been, and insecticide costs, 150 percent greater. Ibid., 28–30.

53. IFDP interview, Tegucigalpa, Honduras, July 1986.

cashews competitive on the world market, the peasants were forced to accept only $7.50. Having been encouraged to shift from corn to cashews, one farmer bitterly told us, "Cashews can be a family's appetizer, but you can't make a meal of them."[54]

In many different countries AID is promoting the same crops, apparently unaware that what happened with broccoli in Guatemala could just as likely happen elsewhere—both within a country and in international trade—if many farmers simultaneously adopt a particular crop.

Finally, what is to guarantee that these products will be allowed to enter the industrialized countries—their main export market—unrestricted?[55] Economic stagnation in the United States and Europe only increases the likelihood that imports will be restricted. In typical understatement, the World Bank and the IMF note that "there is not always a good match between the trade policies urged on recipients and donors' own trade policies, some of which have become increasingly protectionist in recent years."[56]

What Is Development?

Clearly the Reagan administration's revival of discredited development theories cannot end hunger and poverty. Even during the 1970s, when basic human needs received the

---

54. Ibid.

55. Unprocessed oranges from Central America, for example, are barred from the United States because of fear of introducing the Mediterranean fruit fly and the generally low quality of the fruit. The oranges must first be processed into concentrate. Small growers are most affected by this restriction because they have greater difficulty finding a processor to buy their oranges. Most of the processing plants which do exist are owned by *gringos,* according to Dr. Larry Jackson of the Florida Department of Citrus. They tend to have their own trees and are less likely to want the fruit of small farmers. Interview: Sept. 1986.

56. The Development Committee of the World Bank and the IMF, "Aid For Development: The Key Issues," Supporting Material for the Report of the Task Force on Concessional Flows, (Washington, D.C.: The World Bank, Fall 1985), 67–8.

greatest attention within AID, one project after another failed to reach the poorest people. Why do so many official development projects go awry? The answer cannot be found without examining the underlying causes and cures for poverty.

As AID sees it, the poor are poor because they lack certain things: irrigation, credit, better seeds, good roads, or what have you. But we ask: *why* are they lacking these things? The reason is that the poor lack power, power to secure what they need. Identifying the problem as a lack of resources, official aid seeks to bring in from the outside what is missing locally. Yet, we have found that, frequently, the resources needed are available locally. And those resources brought in by official aid invariably end up in the hands of elites, better equipping them to usurp the labor and dwindling resources of the poor.

The official diagnosis assumes that the poor are living in static backwardness and that foreign aid's function is to get things moving by offering material incentives and other benevolent prods. But in most third-world villages the obstacle to positive change is not backwardness, but fear—the legitimate fear among the poor of the brutality of those more powerful. Progress is also thwarted by the severe constraints on production built into hierarchical, often quasi-feudal social structures.[57]

While prevailing development theory sees stagnation and backwardness in third-world countries, in fact people throughout these countries are working to achieve genuine development, often beginning with demands for fair access to farmland.

---

57. For an explanation of how antidemocratic social structures constrain production, see, for example, Frances Moore Lappé and Joseph Collins with Cary Fowler, *Food First: Beyond the Myth of Scarcity* (New York: Ballantine, 1979), pt. 5.

THE INVISIBLE ROOTS OF DEVELOPMENT

Unfortunately, these movements are invisible to most of us living in the industrial countries. Even those initiatives right in our own hometowns often go unseen. Because the initiatives of the poor do not make news, we come to see development only as what happens after outside aid dollars and expertise arrive on the scene.

Thus one major program of our Institute is to learn about the varied efforts among the world's most disadvantaged people to define development for themselves.[58] Many defy the official prescriptions of aid donors. Some of these movements use outside aid, but many are coming to see that foreign aid can only help if they themselves control the direction of their own development. Here we can only give a flavor of the tens of thousands of such initiatives:

The Self-Employed Women's Association (SEWA).[59]   In Ahmedabad City, India, 22,000 poor women—small vendors, seamstresses, trash collectors, and farm laborers—have set up their own credit system and workers' unions to free themselves from dependence on unscrupulous moneylenders and employers. Founded just fifteen years ago, their organization now runs a child-care center, a maternity and health insurance plan, and a housing project.

Along with real material changes in women's lives, organization has brought profound changes in their attitudes and expectations. Chandaben, a member of SEWA, put it this way:

---

58. The program is called "Development That Works." For a compilation of some of its early findings see: *Seeds,* vol. 9, no. 8, Aug. 1986, and the *Food Monitor,* Spring 1986, no. 36.

59. Medea Benjamin, "SEWA: Indian Women Organize," *Seeds,* 15–16. See also Benjamin's forthcoming book *Turning the Tables on Development* to be published by the Institute for Food and Development Policy, Food First Books, in 1988.

My attitude has also changed in so many ways. Before I used to quarrel all the time with my neighbors and relatives over small things—children, water, animals, spilling garbage. These things seemed very great, but now I see they are not worth quarreling over. Now I try to convince our neighbors not to quarrel over little things. I have become more tolerant toward people of other castes. In our public meetings we all sit together and eat together.

The 6-S Association in West Africa.[60] In recent years, villagers in West Africa have begun to appreciate the wealth of their traditional social structures, devalued or destroyed by colonialism. From their efforts have emerged 2,000 peasant groups in some 1,000 villages throughout Burkina Faso, Mali, and Senegal. ("6-S" comes from French words which mean "using the dry season in the Savannah and the Sahel.")

Founder of 6-S, Bernard Ouedraogo believes that a lost tradition—*Naam*—can be the key to solving today's problems in his homeland. Created centuries ago by the Mossi in Burkina Faso, Naam brings the village youth—from age eight to thirty-five—together in groups to work cooperatively, learning from the elders how to carry on the Mossi traditions. Explained Ouedraogo:

Everyone within Naam is considered equal; the rich have no more say than the poor, women are equal to men. No one dominates anyone else. That is the cooperative essence of Naam. When the young people "graduate" at age 35, they are not perfect people, but they know how to live together and to share with others.

In his response to outside aid, Ouedraogo stressed the need for patience: "The villages we work with have to organize and

---

60. Medea Benjamin, "A Mossi Must Always Use Two Hands of His Own," *Seeds*. 27–28.

work for two, three, sometimes up to ten years before they receive any outside aid at all." But most of all he underscored the need for self-direction. "Aid is only useful if the will is there," he told our staff. "When aid arrives before the organization is consolidated, it can do more harm than good."

A dramatic metaphor summed up the 6-S approach to outside aid. "Our philosophy is very simple," said Ouedraogo. "If an outsider is willing to come and help us by grabbing the bull's tail, that's great. But we're the ones who have to grab the bull by the horns." In other words, outsiders might participate, but only after local people have firmly established their own needs and goals.

DEVELOPMENT, A SOCIAL PROCESS

In more than a decade of struggling to formulate a definition of development, we have had to distinguish development from growth and productivity. We have seen that it is possible to have more growth while, at the same time, the poor majority become poorer and more desperate for survival.[61]

Thus, for us, *genuine* development—development that enhances opportunities for all people to realize their potential—must involve change in the relationships among people, which in turn determine their access to productive resources. Development is not a technical but a social process, in which people join together to build economic and political institutions serving the interests of the majority. In that process, more and more people unite to acquire the knowledge and techniques they need to develop their resources and to free themselves from hunger, disease, and ignorance.

When the U.S. aid establishment tries to sell development assistance to Congress, it has a very different definition of development in mind. It stresses that foreign aid's benefits

---

61. For a discussion of contrasting definitions of development, see Guy Gran, *Development By People: Citizen Construction of a Just World* (New York: Praeger, 1983).

accrue to U.S. firms, since the bulk of our aid dollars end up purchasing U.S. goods and services. But if we perceive development as a process of profound social change, our perception of U.S. interests changes also. Policymakers in Washington believe that U.S. companies can benefit from the keep-the-lid-on-change foreign policy charted in our previous two chapters. The unspoken assumption is that protecting the status quo means protecting the business interests and well-off consumers abroad who are most likely to buy U.S. goods.

Such a narrow and shortsighted view of U.S. interests reflects a failure to imagine economic development in which the vast majority of people are able to realize their hopes for better food, farming equipment, housing, schooling, clothing, and so on. As long as change in this direction is thwarted, U.S. companies may be able to continue selling tractors to the richest landowners, or whiskey and cosmetics to the urban upper classes, but they are denied the immeasurably greater markets for basic goods, markets that are missing today because hundreds of millions of people are too poor to express their basic needs as demand in the marketplace.

Development assistance—that small portion of U.S. aid actually targeted to development projects—could only serve this more long-term and broader definition of development if it were to support initiatives for change controlled by the poor themselves, like those highlighted above. But to support such efforts on a significant scale would pit AID against the interests of the elites dominating most governments abroad. To do so would entail going headlong against the formidable lobbyists of the handful of multinational corporations which reap the bulk of the profit from U.S. aid. To do so would risk supporting economic alternatives abroad involving greater participation by farmers and workers that might lead more Americans to question the fairness of their own economic system. Obviously, no U.S. government agency is about to do so.

For this reason, we conclude that whether AID is pushing its 1970s New Directions program or backsliding to the trickle-down strategies of the 1960s, it cannot arrive at an effective diagnosis of the root causes of underdevelopment— one in which the issue of control over resources is central— until changes are underway here at home. First, Americans must reshape our government's definition of our national interest so that it will not be threatened by thoroughgoing change in the third world. We return to this theme in our concluding chapter.

Four

U.S. Food Aid:
Weapon Against Hunger?

IN 1984, Haitian peasants in a remote village angrily waved machetes at helicopters attempting to land nearby, helicopters loaded not with weapons but with U.S. food aid. This scene was one sign of the intense controversy surrounding what on the surface appears to be a strictly benevolent act. Scratch that surface, however, and many tough questions emerge: Does an influx of food aid undercut prices local farmers get, making it even harder for them to stay in business? Is government-to-government food aid just another form of economic support offered to keep friendly regimes afloat?

Most Americans aren't aware of such questions because they assume that most U.S. food aid responds to famine emergencies. This is hardly surprising, since Americans voluntarily donated over $100 million to African relief in the mid-eighties and as taxpayers contributed over a billion dollars to such aid in 1985 alone.[1] But in a typical year, only about *one-tenth* of

---

1. This figure refers to 1985, and comes from "Africa Drought Report: Famine Eases, But Needs Still Exist in 1986," AID news release, no. 0012, Office of Press Relations, Mar. 11, 1986. Despite its ultimate show of generosity, the U.S. govern-

U.S. food aid is used for emergency, famine-relief operations. What happens to the less visible ninety percent? The bulk is not given away; it is sold to foreign governments.

Food Aid Sales

Over the last thirty years, sixty percent of all U.S. food aid has been shipped abroad under a program called Title I of Public Law 480—or P.L. 480, as it is widely known.[2] Under Title I, the U.S. government provides low interest loans to selected governments to purchase our surplus agricultural commodities. These governments then resell the food in their domestic markets as they see fit, with the revenue from sales going into the national treasury.[3] In Bangladesh, for example, most of the food is sold in the urban areas at the market price and to the military at one-fifth the market price, while food subsidies for the poor are being cut back.[4] Most of our food aid cannot reach hungry people; they simply are too poor to buy it.

Why would the United States sell food aid instead of giving it away?

In part, the answer is that boosting sales abroad of U.S. farm commodities has been one of the primary, stated purposes of

ment was painfully slow in recognizing and responding to the crisis. Though aware of the famine as early as 1982, the government did not send U.S. food aid until well into 1983. The major portion of food assistance was delivered in 1985, some three years after learning of the problem. See U.S. General Accounting Office, *Famine in Africa: Improving Emergency Food Relief Programs,* report no. GAO/NSIAD-86-25 (Washington D.C.: U.S. GAO, Mar. 1986).

2. Calculated from *U.S. Overseas Loans and Grants and Assistance from International Organizations, July 1, 1945–Sept. 30, 1985* (Washington, D.C.: Agency for International Development), 4.

3. Some countries do maintain a separate account for P.L. 480 funds. Even in these cases, however, the recipient can spend the proceeds as it pleases, as long as the use of the money conforms to the broadly defined U.S. requirement of "contributing to development."

4. IFDP interview with David Kinley of the U.N. Development Programme, after research in Bangladesh in mid-1986.

U.S. food aid from its very inception. Humanitarian aims were not explicitly incorporated into the program until 1966, twelve years after it began.[5]

FOOD AID AS SURPLUS DISPOSAL

P.L. 480 arose from a problem still plaguing American agriculture: tremendous grain surpluses. During the 1940s, U.S. grain production to support the war effort grew by leaps and bounds. Chemical fertilizers, pesticides, and improved seed varieties, along with government price supports, had pushed crop yields up.[6] And after the war, these extra food supplies helped feed war-devastated Europe. (Some historians note, however, that America's use of emergency food aid for political ends actually began in this period.)[7]

But by the early 1950s, European nations were back on their feet, and they no longer needed (or wanted) American food. Increased domestic demand wasn't nearly enough to absorb the expanded supply of grain; just storing excess food was costing American taxpayers nearly $1 million a day.[8]

Surely there were millions of hungry people here and abroad who could have benefited from cheaper food, but neither the farm lobby nor the giant grain-trading corporations wanted the surpluses flooding the market, pushing prices down. At its national convention in 1952, the American Farm

5. For historical background on the U.S. food aid program, see Mitchel B. Wallerstein, *Food For War, Food for Peace* (Cambridge, Mass.: MIT Press, 1980), esp. chapter 3; and the International Trade and Development Education Foundation, *The United States Food For Peace Program, 1954–84.* Spring 1985.

6. See also *Food First: Beyond the Myth of Scarcity* by Frances Moore Lappé and Joseph Collins with Cary Fowler (New York: Ballantine Books, 1979), and *Aid As Obstacle* by Frances Moore Lappé, Joseph Collins, and David Kinley (San Francisco: Food First Books, 1981).

7. Gabriel Kolko, *The Politics of War: The World and United States Foreign Policy, 1943–1945* (New York: Random House, 1968), 496–499.

8. Today, the cost of storing surplus agricultural commodities is far higher: $1.85 million per day. Interview with Shirlene Williams of the U.S. Department of Agriculture, Oct. 1986.

Bureau, representing large and medium-sized farmers, proposed a clever solution: allow food-deficit countries to pay for U.S. food imports *in their own currencies* instead of in hard-to-earn American dollars. Then, poor third-world governments could begin buying surplus American food, while not undercutting commercial food prices charged to higher-income countries. The idea caught on, and in 1954, the P.L. 480 food aid program was born.

SURPLUS DISPOSAL AND THE NEEDS OF THE POOR

P.L. 480 food sales abroad appeared to be one of those rare instances in which everyone wins—U.S. farmers, U.S. grain traders, third-world governments, and the hungry overseas. But the "everyone wins" view is grounded in a key misunderstanding of the reason why so many go hungry in the first place.

It presumes that the cause of hunger is a shortage of food and food-producing potential, a gap that must be filled with shipments from abroad. But many of the countries to which we ship food aid are actually *exporters* of agricultural commodities themselves, a trading pattern imposed upon them by a colonizing power. Six of the top ten recipients of U.S. food aid were *net* exporters of agricultural commodities in 1983, meaning they exported more than they imported. (This is the most recent year for which trade data are available.)[9]

Since agricultural exports include many non-nutritious items like coffee and cocoa, we are not saying that current food production could in every case meet the entire people's needs. But these exports suggest that the resources may well exist to

9. Data on U.S. food aid recipients come from U.S. Agency for International Development, *Congressional Presentation, Fiscal Year 1985,* main vol., and refer to Titles I, II, and III combined (excluding emergency assistance) for 1983. Data on net exports come from *U.N. Food and Agriculture Organization, Trade Yearbook, 1983* (Rome: FAO, 1984), table 6. Net agricultural exporters in 1983 (by value) include India, Pakistan, Indonesia, Sudan, El Salvador, and Sri Lanka.

provide food for everyone, if more of those resources were devoted to local food production. Moreover, several major food aid recipients are already producing surpluses of food. By 1986, one of the biggest headaches of the Indian government was 30 million tons of surplus grain, costing half a billion dollars to store.[10]

Enough food is being produced, or could be grown, to feed everyone in virtually every country where hunger is now widespread.[11] What the poor lack is access to farmland and tools needed to grow the food, or the money to buy food. In countries where enough food is already grown, obviously our aid is not filling a food-deficit gap. When sold by the government, it serves instead as a source of government revenue. When it is given away in long-term feeding programs, food aid allows the recipient government to postpone reform, reform that could enable people now receiving handouts to become customers for the already existing production of their own country.

A second error within the notion that everyone benefits from food aid is that the basic law of supply and demand is forgotten. Contrary to some people's prejudice, food aid does not make people lazy. Much worse, it actually can undermine their capacity to provide for themselves. When we flood their markets with cheap, American food we undercut the prices that local farmers can charge for their products—sometimes to the point where they can't even cover their production costs.[12]

---

10. Title I food aid to India stopped as of 1978, but India still receives large quantities of Title II food commodities which we describe below.

11. See *Food First* by Lappé, Collins, and Fowler and *World Hunger: Twelve Myths* by Frances Moore Lappé and Joseph Collins (San Francisco and New York: Food First Books/Grove Press, 1986).

12. See, for example: L. Dudley and R. J. Sandilands, "The Side Effects of Foreign Aid: The Case of P.L. 480 Wheat in Colombia," *Economic Development and Cultural Change,* vol. 23, Jan. 1975, 325–336, and P. J. Isenman and H. W. Singer, "Food Aid: Disincentive Effects and Their Policy Implications," *Economic Development and Cultural Change,* vol. 25, no. 2, Jan. 1977, 205–237. Yet another type of disincentive is price uncertainty farmers face due to lack of coordination by food aid donors. See D. Bigman, *Food Policies and Food Security Under Instability: Modeling and Analysis* (Lexington, Mass.: Lexington Books, 1985).

AID has been aware of this disincentive effect since the early 1960s.[13] Yet not until 1977 did Congress require governments receiving food aid for resale to certify that its distribution will not undercut local producers and marketers.[14] But the distribution of food aid has been little affected. Not a single country has been refused Title I funds on these grounds.[15]

So U.S. food aid continues to undercut local farmers. Here are a few examples:

Central America. In the early 1980s, the ministers of agriculture of the four Central American countries receiving U.S. food aid were upset that P.L. 480 corn was flooding their markets and depressing prices.[16] In a meeting with then U.S. Secretary of Agriculture John R. Block, they said that if the United States really wanted to help Central America, it should buy the food for its aid programs from farmers in the region. Block allegedly replied, "But that won't help our producers."[17]

Apparently the agricultural ministers' opposition was overridden by their governments' interest in other benefits from food aid. Between 1982 and 1985, the United States sent several hundred thousand tons of corn to Central America.[18]

The Caribbean. Large shipments of U.S. food aid have so depressed market prices in Haiti that farmers are reluctant to bring their crops to market the week that food aid

---

13. "A Comparative Analysis of Five P.L. 480 Title I Impact Evaluation Studies," AID Program Evaluation Discussion Paper, no. 19, Dec. 1983, x.

14. Ibid., 9.

15. Interview with Mary Chambliss of the USDA, July 1986.

16. This group includes Honduras, El Salvador, Costa Rica and Guatemala.

17. Interview with a U.N. official, who wishes to remain anonymous, June 1986.

18. Calculated from unpublished data contained in "The Exports Under P.L. 480," provided to us by the U.S. Food for Peace Office, Washington, D.C., June 1986. This figure of 380,000 metric tons represents a significant underestimate in that it only includes Title II corn exports for the last year of the period, namely, 1985. Data for Titles I and III cover the whole period, however.

arrives.[19] But increasing dependence on food aid doesn't concern AID; in fact, it is part of AID's plan for shifting almost a third of Haiti's farmland from producing food to producing for export. AID argues that the export crops include tree crops like coffee, which will help prevent soil loss on Haiti's seriously eroded land. So, if food aid depresses food prices, so much the better—farmers will be encouraged to shift out of subsistence crops.[20]

But Haitian farmers are not pleased. In 1984, rice farmers in Les Cayes chased away helicopters bearing U.S. aid rice by massing at the landing zone brandishing their machetes. On a research trip in late 1986, we spoke with many angry peasant farmers who complained that U.S. food aid was undercutting the prices for their products and driving them out of business.

And in Jamaica, "heavy dumping of surplus food has glutted markets, driven down prices . . . and discouraged local production," concludes the author of a 1986 study of foreign aid.[21]

Somalia. In 1984, U.S. food aid was being sold at prices as little as one-sixth the local market prices. Diplomatic ties between the United States and the Somalian government were cemented, and urban consumers gained, concludes an AID review, but the cheaper food hurt farmers.[22]

This disincentive effect of food aid on local producers is hotly debated.[23] Some argue that in most cases food aid im-

---

19. Based on the testimony of a development consultant before the House Subcommittee on Foreign Operations. Cited in *The Wall Street Journal*, "Free Food Bankrupts Foreign Farmers," July 2, 1984.

20. Josh DeWind and David Kinley, *Aiding Migration*, 137, 141–142.

21. James Bovard, "A Costly Cover for a Failing Policy," *The New York Times*, Nov. 23, 1986, 2F. Bovard's study is for the *Journal of Economic Growth*.

22. U.S. AID Mission to Somalia, "An Evaluation of the United States Government's Title I Food Aid Program to Somalia," Sept. 1984, 65, 67.

23. E. J. Clay and H. W. Singer "Food Aid and Development: Issues and Evidence" (a survey of the the literature since 1977 on the role and impact of food aid in developing countries), Occasional Papers, no. 3, World Program, Public Affairs and Information Unit, Via dell Terme di Caracalla, 00100 Rome, Italy, especially chapter 3.

ports are too small to affect market prices. And some investigators claim that even if they do, it's worth it: reduced prices resulting from food aid means that the poor are able to buy more, a benefit outweighing any other consideration.[24] But whether the poor gain from lower prices depends on whether they are net buyers of food who find their purchasing power raised, or net sellers whose incomes are hurt. In many countries, most rural poor are net sellers of food.

Others point out that a government could use the proceeds from the sale of food aid directly to support poor farmers, through price or credit subsidies. True enough, if governments felt accountable to the poor. But in most countries, it is largely because governments are *un*accountable to their poor, especially poor rural people, that food aid is needed in the first place!

Let us explain by taking up the second and, we believe, less debatable point regarding the disincentives that food aid provides: food aid undercuts the government's incentive for reform.

Food Aid: Reprieve Against Reform

Cheap, imported food can allow a government to leave unaddressed the real causes for stagnant production of basic foods. First, by relying on food aid, it can keep prices miserably low for subsistence food crops, thus ensuring low production.

Second, food aid allows a government to leave the rural elite's stranglehold over productive resources intact, even though big landowners typically use · their resources less effectively and are more likely to shift to export crops than small farmers. In other words, when Title I commodities become a dependable and cheap source of food, governments

---

24. See for example: John W. Mellor, "Food Aid and Nutrition," *American Journal of Agricultural Economics,* vol. 62, no. 5, Dec. 1980.

beholden to big landowners find it easier to put off reform. They can postpone challenging the resource monopoly of the better-off, a step needed to release the productive potential of the land.

Bangladesh.   For more than a decade, a steady stream of (largely U.S.) food aid has flowed to Bangladesh. Although food production has increased somewhat in the 1980s, investment in agriculture remains low.

More than half of all rural Bangladeshis are deprived of land, yet the government refuses to enforce two land reform measures that could move the country toward a fairer landholding pattern, necessary to tap the country's rich potential.[25] With grain yields lagging well behind the Asian average, Bangladesh's striking agricultural potential has hardly been developed.

Tanzania.   In 1984, Tanzania's fertile regions produced enough food to feed the entire population *and* provide a surplus of more than 100,000 tons.[26] But much of this food made its way out of the country illegally, because traders could sell it in nearby Burundi and Kenya for three times the price offered by the Tanzanian government. That same year, the Tanzanian government asked donor agencies (including AID) for 200,000 tons of food to meet consumer demand, especially for wheat.[27] Could the government's access to cheap food imports be in part what has allowed it to pay its farmers such low prices?

---

25. See U.S. AID *Congressional Presentation. FY 1986.* Asia vol., 25. For an excellent overview of rural realities in Bangladesh, see Betsy Hartmann and James Boyce, *A Quiet Violence* (San Francisco: Food First Books, 1983).

26. Cited in Paula Park and Tony Jackson, *Lands of Plenty, Lands of Scarcity: Agricultural Policy and Peasant Farmers in Zimbabwe and Tanzania* (Oxford, U.K.: Oxfam, Apr. 1985), 11, 13.

27. Ibid., 12, 14.

Egypt. For many years, U.S.-supplied food aid has allowed the Egyptian government to keep the price of wheat products down, but at the expense of farmers. The price that the government has been paying farmers is so low that "domestically produced wheat may be assigned more value as fodder for animals and in brick making than for human consumption."[28] Not surprisingly, few Egyptian farmers even bother marketing wheat today.

With better prices, however, there's little doubt that the Egyptian farmer would respond. When P.L. 480 wheat shipments were cut off because of the Egypt-Israeli War in 1967, the Egyptian government was forced to raise its procurement prices to stimulate wheat output. By 1975, domestic wheat production had climbed forty-three percent.[29]

We should take care, however, not to overstate the importance of price to third-world farmers. In order to increase production, farmers need more than a fair price. They need land; they need credit to purchase tools and other inputs; they need the certainty of markets for their increased output; they need consumer goods available to buy with their new cash income. All of these additional prerequisites to increased output hinge on a far-reaching redirection of government policies, *none* of which food aid in itself encourages.

Building A Market

Getting rid of surpluses through concessional sales abroad is only part of the original purpose—and continuing function—of P.L. 480. It "is a bill to promote trade . . ." stated one of

---

28. *P.L. 480 Title I: The Egyptian Case,* AID Project Impact Evaluation Report, no. 45, June 1983, x.

29. Ibid., 7.

its staunch supporters, Senator Andrew Shoepple, in 1954. "In no sense does the bill provide for a giveaway program."[30]

Promoters of P.L. 480 argued that by introducing U.S. agricultural products into third-world diets, people would develop a taste for our exports, thereby becoming a future *commercial* market, paying full price. And for some higher-income countries, this is exactly what has happened. Currently eight of the top ten customers of U.S. farm products are former recipients of U.S. food aid, boasts the Department of Agriculture.[31]

South Korea is AID's prize example of an "aid to trade" success story. Between 1956 and 1981, food aid to South Korea totaled $1.6 billion. Since "graduating" from the food aid program in 1981, South Korea has become a major importer of U.S. agricultural commodities, despite impressive improvements in yields per acre. South Korea now purchases over $2 billion in U.S. farm commodities each year.[32]

What have been the consequences of this success? In 1985, the Korean Christian Farmers' organization wrote about their plight in an open letter to President Reagan:

> Due to the flooding of foreign agricultural products into Korea, our farmers have suffered chronic deficits in their farming operations, causing them to go deeper and deeper into debt. . . . [Of] these foreign agricultural goods which are destroying Korean agriculture and our farmers' livelihood, 90 percent or more are exported from the United States.[33]

---

30. International Trade and Development Education Foundation, *The United States Food For Peace Program, 1954–84.* Spring 1985, 6.

31. United States Department of Agriculture, *Food for Peace: 1984 Annual Report on Public Law 480* (Washington, D.C.: USDA, July 1985), 1.

32. "AID Policies, Priorities and the Private Sector," Address by M. Peter McPherson, Administrator of AID to the Washington International Business Council, Jan. 20, 1984, 2.

33. *Global Food Disorder.* Resource Packet for Churches, World Council of Churches, Geneva, May 1986.

While food aid had helped South Korea forty years ago, American farm commodities have continued to pour in while "Korea's income from its own crops such as wheat and cotton has dropped," the farmers lament. Meeting all its own food needs just twenty-five years ago, South Korea now imports half its grain supply and seventy percent of its soybean consumption.[34] "Our former self-sufficiency is being lost," write the farmers, and, "many people are beginning to doubt whether the U.S. is truly our closest free-world ally."[35]

Moreover, these soybean imports go largely to produce meat products that the poor in South Korea cannot afford. In fact, over half of U.S. food exports go to produce livestock products which the world's poor never eat.

Concern over markets for U.S. products also shapes food aid to Africa. In 1986, Zimbabwe wanted to ship its surplus white maize (corn) to neighboring Mozambique, which had been scheduled to get U.S. yellow maize as food aid. (In exchange, Zimbabwe would get an equivalent amount of U.S. wheat.) AID protested. An agency official explained that such an arrangement would harm AID's own goal "to make the people of southern Africa change their preference from white maize to yellow maize in order to create a market for U.S. yellow maize." AID prevailed: only a tenth of Mozambique's food aid that year came as white maize from Zimbabwe.[36]

P.L. 480's designers turned out to be correct in their hunch that people's food tastes could be easily changed—especially when the foods that we export—wheat and feed to produce meat—are linked in consumers' minds with what's modern and Western. In many parts of Asia, where people traditionally ate rice, wheat is now a staple food. Similarly, in many

---

34. IFDP interview with the Agricultural Attaché, Korean Embassy, Washington, D.C., June 1986.

35. *Global Food Disorder.*

36. Carol B. Thompson, "SADCC's Struggle for Economic Liberation," *Africa Report,* July–Aug. 1986, 63.

Central American cities, white bread is rapidly displacing traditional corn tortillas.[37]

We ponder the long-range consequences of populations demanding a diet which cannot be produced locally. For a dependency on food imports can make governments vulnerable not only to unpredictable international markets but to political manipulation by food-exporting nations as well.

In our opening chapter, we argued that the vast majority of Americans and most people living in the third world share common interests. But if many third-world people would gain from greater food self-reliance, don't their interests collide with American farmers' need for ever larger export markets?

During the 1970s, the dependency of U.S. farmers on export markets doubled. By the end of the decade, one-third of farm income came from sales abroad. But this export boom did not bring farmers sustained prosperity; it helped precipitate the worst farm depression since the 1930s. Export markets are notoriously fickle. Moreover, U.S. policies to boost exports have accelerated the depletion of the topsoil and groundwater (for irrigation) needed by future generations. We are already losing topsoil faster than nature can replenish it on one-third of American farmland. So we ask: might not American farmers—and ultimately all Americans—gain by not more but less dependence on export markets?[38] Given the unparalleled agricultural endowment of the United States, we could conserve our soil and water resources and still continue significant exports. However, avoiding overdependency on foreign markets is in the interest of both our farmers and the land itself.

There is yet another layer of complexity to the common interests issue as it relates to agricultural trade. Once societies

---

37. Food aid is not solely responsible for changing food tastes and eating habits: the exposure to imports associated with urbanization is also an important factor. There can be little doubt that food aid has significantly contributed to the process, however.

38. For a full discussion of these issues, see James Wessel with Mort Hantman, *Trading the Future* (San Francisco: Institute for Food and Development Policy, 1983).

are on the path of broad-based development, in which land and credit reform is pushing up food production and the vast majority of people are making income gains, an increase in food imports is likely, even if local production goes up. Trade offers the enjoyment of greater food variety. Thus, whether considering the American farmers' need to be less vulnerable to international markets or their need for ongoing customers, the interests of our farmers do not oppose those of most third-world producers and consumers.

Food aid is often used as a substitute for broad-based reform in the third world, as we have seen. To a lesser extent, the same case might be made here at home: to the degree that food aid is justified to American farmers by the promise of building future commercial markets, it diverts attention from the need for far-reaching reform of *our* farm programs. Neither the crisis of soil erosion nor the crisis of family farm bankruptcies can be solved by a narrow emphasis on greater farm sales abroad.

Food as a Weapon

With proper use these surpluses can be made a far more potent means of combating the spread of Communism than the hydrogen bomb.

—CONGRESSMAN CLIFFORD R. HOPE, JUNE 15, 1954[39]

I think this bill will have a great impact on the conduct of our policy in foreign affairs, in that food can be used as a weapon. I say to you, Mr. Chairman, we have never made the use of food as a weapon as effectively as we should in this fight against the insidious effects of Communism.

—CONGRESSMAN FRED MARSHALL, JUNE 15, 1954.[40]

39. Congressional Record, June 15, 1954. Quoted in International Trade and Development Education Foundation, *The United States Food For Peace Program. 1954–84.* 8.

40. Ibid.

From the passage of P.L. 480, food aid has been distributed largely to reward allies, not to respond to need. In Chart 8 you'll see that fully two-thirds of all P.L. 480 commodities goes to just ten countries.[41] And fewer than *half* of these countries are designated "low income" by the World Bank.

CHART 8: TOP TEN RECIPIENTS OF U.S.
FOOD AID IN 1985
($ millions)

Country	P.L. 480 Food Aid
1. Egypt	$238.2
*2. Bangladesh	113.5
*3. India	90.8
*4. Sudan	64.8
5. Morocco	63.8
*6. Pakistan	59.0
7. El Salvador	52.1
8. Philippines	47.8
9. Indonesia	46.4
10. Dominican Rep.	42.4
Subtotal	$818.8
All Other Countries	427.3
TOTAL	$1246.1

*Country designated as low income by the World Bank, *World Development Report, 1985.*

Source: U.S. Agency for International Development, *Congressional Presentation, Fiscal Year 1987,* 666–668. Data include Titles I, II, and III, and refer to regular country allocations. Centrally programmed aid is excluded.

---

41. Calculated from AID, *Congressional Presentation, FY 1987,* 666–668. (Data refer to 1985, however.) Note that this calculation excludes food aid which was centrally programmed, i.e., supplementally approved food aid to Africa and Central America. This category of aid was specifically excluded because it doesn't represent normal programming and is purely a function of the 1985 famine relief.

Food aid is, in large part, merely another form of economic aid, concentrated on the same governments receiving U.S. assistance in other forms. But because food is a survival necessity, unlike funds to build dams or roads, food can be a powerful weapon to try to bend a foreign government to the donor's will.

To this end, the U.S. government has turned food aid on and off like a spigot—to reward and punish, to carry on wars that don't have full congressional support, and, most recently, to bend recipients to the economic philosophy of Washington policymakers.

Food aid to make a political point

Egypt. Between 1967 and 1974, food aid to Egypt was suspended as punishment for the two Egyptian-Israeli wars fought during that period, and not resumed again until 1976 when Egypt began to show signs of its willingness to begin peace negotiations with Israel.[42]

Peru. Angered by the nationalization of a U.S. oil company, the United States cut off aid to Peru between 1969 and 1974.[43]

---

42. *P.L. 480 Title I: The Egyptian Case*, AID Project Impact Evaluation Report, no. 45, June 1983, 2.

43. See, for instance, "The Impact of P.L. 480 Title I in Peru: Food Aid as an Effective Development Resource," AID Project Impact Evaluation, no. 47, Oct. 1983, 7. Food aid has also been used a way of coaxing policy changes out of a recipient government. In the 1960s, for example, India was forced to accept "one of the hardest bargains for aid ever driven by the U.S. government," according to analysts T. J. Byres and Ben Crow. Shortly after India had entered in to war with Pakistan, the U.S. government called a halt to the second half of its P.L. 480 shipment. Knowing that India was desperate for food imports, it demanded that the Indian government make a number of changes which would benefit U.S. corporations and at the same time further U.S. foreign policy. For example, the government of India had to relinquish its control over fertilizer pricing and distribution by private firms for seven years; drop its demand for fifty-one percent ownership of joint ventures in the fertilizer industry; allow greater latitude to American private firms operating in India; and cut off all trade with North Vietnam. Faced with few other options, the

To fight wars

Indochina.   During the Vietnam War, not only were Vietnam and South Korea slated to receive a disproportionate amount of U.S. food aid—almost half of the total amount by 1974—but eighty percent of the money generated from Title I sales was used to strengthen the South Vietnamese armed forces.[44]

"The priorities governing the Food For Peace program are clear," said Senator Mark Hatfield in 1974. "They are to support economies geared to war, rather than to relieve famine and starvation."[45] The "famine and starvation" to which he referred was in the African Sahel, which at that time was undergoing one of its worst droughts of the century.[46]

Central America.   Today, food aid funds in El Salvador are again being diverted to support a war effort. Since 1982, $187 million in P.L. 480 food aid has been shipped to the government of El Salvador—well over *four times as much food aid per capita as the U.S. government sent to the whole of drought-stricken Africa over the same period.*[47] Half of the proceeds from the sale of these U.S. food aid commodities has been used in the government of El Salvador's pacification program (described in chapter 2), according to a con-

---

Indian government complied. (See T. J. Byres and Ben Crow, "The Green Revolution in India," Case Study Five, The Open University Press, 1983, 27.)

44. International Trade and Development Education Foundation, *The United States Food For Peace Program, 1954–84,* 22.

45. Congressional Record, Dec. 4, 1974. Quoted in *The United States Food For Peace Program, 1954–84,* 23.

46. Food aid to the Sahel during the 1968–73 drought totaled only $54.7 million dollars, less than seven percent of what Vietnam and Cambodia had received over the same period. Calculated from U.S. Overseas Loans and Grants, July 1, 1945, to Sept. 30, 1974.

47. Data refer to the period from 1982–85. Including supplemental appropriations, drought-ravaged Africa received $7.74 per capita, while food aid to El Salvador for the same period was $36.01 per capita. Calculated from AID *Congressional Presentation, FY 1984–87.* See also: *Help or Hindrance? U.S. Economic Aid in Central America* (San Francisco: Institute for Food and Development Policy, 1987).

gressional report.[48] Another quarter has gone to displaced persons uprooted from their homes as a result of the war.[49]

In Guatemala, local currencies generated by U.S. food assistance have been used by the government for its high-security "model" village program to keep tabs on poor peasants, separating them from insurgents. Part of this program has been described as "forced internment" by U.S. observers.[50]

To bend other governments to Washington's economic ideology

Kenya. In 1985, AID held up food shipments for months until the government finally agreed to let the private sector distribute the food. So wedded was the Reagan administration to its private enterprise philosophy that it would not listen to Kenyan officials who explained that no one outside of government had the expertise to handle the millions of tons of food aid.[51]

Dominican Republic. Although eighty people died in food riots in 1984 in the Dominican Republic, AID officials in 1986 insisted that the government abolish its food purchasing agency in favor of the private sector before rice could be shipped under P.L. 480.[52]

48. "U.S. Aid to El Salvador: An Evaluation of the Past, A Proposal for the Future," a report to the Arms Control and Foreign Policy Caucus from Representatives Jim Leach, George Miller, and Senator Mark Hatfield, Feb. 1985, 20.

49. Ibid., 20.

50. Chris Krueger, Kjell Enge, *Security and Development Conditions in the Guatemalan Highlands,* Washington Office on Latin America, Washington, D.C., 1985, viii.

51. Jack Anderson and Joseph Spear, "Ideology and Famine Relief," *The Washington Post,* July 29, 1986.

52. Ibid.

The New Face of Food Aid?

Over the years many Americans have struggled to shift the focus of food aid toward alleviating hunger and contributing to development. In 1975, Congress passed a new foreign assistance bill requiring that three-quarters of Title I food aid go to countries where annual per capita GNP was $300 or less.[53]

Two years later, new amendments went even further: Title I food aid was to be denied to any "country which engages in a consistent pattern of gross violations of internationally recognized human rights," and a new Food For Development program (known as Title III) was created. Under Food for Development, food aid loans can be forgiven if a government pledges to use the proceeds to boost its own agricultural production, or to "improve the quality of rural life" through health, nutrition, and family planning programs.[54] Then in 1982, to put some teeth into these provisions, the Gilman-Solarz legislation required that the self-help measures which qualified governments for loan forgiveness be "specific and measurable."

But these initiatives to reform food aid have neither succeeded in mitigating its negative effects nor in getting food aid to the hungry. Examining each legislative reform, even briefly, we can see why each fails to come to grips with food aid's inherent contradictions. Let's start with the 1975 rule directing the bulk of our food aid to the poorest countries, measured by per capita GNP—and by extension, it was assumed, to the poorest people.

Its effectiveness was undermined from the onset by the bill's assumption that per capita output tells us something about the extent of hunger. It cannot. Peru's per capita GNP is $1,040,

53. According to the main volume of the *Congressional Presentation FY 1987*, the limit is currently $790.

54. Title III eligibility is limited to those countries with a per capita GNP of $790 per year or less.

yet over half the children under age six suffer from chronic malnutrition.[55] The Chinese per capita GNP, by contrast, is $300; yet few Chinese citizens go without at least a minimally adequate diet. Cuba's per capita GNP is lower than South Africa's, but while the majority of South Africans are undernourished (almost all of them black), Cuba's nutrition problems result from overeating and bad dietary habits, not lack of food. GNP per capita is no measure of hunger.

Second, the GNP criterion overlooks altogether the question of whether a government will use food aid to alleviate hunger—in other words, whether the recipient government is accountable to its people. Haiti is one of the poorest countries in the world, and has been a prime candidate for aid under these rules. But its deposed president, Jean Claude Duvalier, siphoned off millions of dollars' worth of U.S. food aid for his own personal gain.[56] Similarly, Somalia, with a per capita GNP of $250 a year, easily qualifies for U.S. food aid. But the government of Somalia allocates eighty percent of Title I commodities to the military and government employees.[57] Its food aid is rarely seen by the poor.

Like the GNP criterion, the amendment denying Title I food aid to gross human rights violators sounds strong. But it contains a gaping loophole: the recipient government can simply sign a clause vouching that the food aid will directly (or indirectly, through its resale) help the needy, and the prohibition is promptly lifted. It is not too surprising that *U.S. food aid has never been denied to any country because of its human rights record.*[58]

---

55. Data on Peru's per capita GNP come from the World Bank, *World Development Report, 1985,* table 1, while data on its malnutrition come from AID *Congressional Presentation, FY 1988,* Annex III, Latin America and the Caribbean, p. 348, and exclude those living in Lima.

56. "Duvalier Accused of Graft on Food," *The New York Times,* Mar. 18, 1986, 18.

57. AID Mission to Somalia, "An Evaluation of the United States Government's Title I Food Aid Program to Somalia," Sept. 1984, 67.

58. Information furnished by Vita Bite at the Congressional Research Service, correspondence dated Jan. 15, 1986. According to Ms. Bite, the Inter-Agency Group

The Food for Development Program (Title III) in which U.S. food aid loans are forgiven if proceeds of food aid sales go to specified development projects, has also had little impact. In its first seven years (1977–1984), only six[59] countries had agreed to sign Title III agreements.[60] Why so few? A General Accounting Office evaluation suggests that, apparently, not many governments are willing to forego the budgetary leeway they currently have under Title I in exchange for loan forgiveness.[61]

Even if more governments were to use Food for Development funds—submitting to restrictions on the use of proceeds from food aid sales—the negative effects of food aid, including the undercutting of local farmers by commodity sales on the open market, would still remain.

Finally, what has come of the tough Gilman-Solarz agreements, meant to tie governments to *specific* self-help measures? Originally designed to encourage greater food production, the actual amendment includes numerous provisions going far beyond this goal. They include, for example, the shifting of land into the production of needed food, and the provision of training and technical assistance to farmers (including programs to reduce illiteracy).[62]

Most of these "strings" sound very constructive, but the Reagan administration has been highly selective in pulling them. It has focused almost exclusively on those parts of the bill specifying government policy reform, especially incentives to private enterprise.

Pakistan's self-help agreements are typical. They stipulate:

---

on Human Rights and Foreign Assistance may place countries warranting human rights concern on a special list. As of Jan. 1986, the five countries on this list were Zaire, Indonesia, Guatemala, the Philippines, and Haiti.

59. Countries which have signed Title III Agreements are: Sudan, Senegal, Egypt, Bangladesh, Bolivia, and Honduras. Honduras had signed an agreement at one point but later terminated it and now plans to start up again.

60. U.S. GAO, *Financial and Management Improvements Needed in the Food For Development Program* (Washington, D.C.: U.S. GAO, Aug. 7, 1985), i.

61. Ibid., 4.

62. *Food for Peace: 1984 Annual Report,* 10.

- decreasing government subsidies for consumers;
- promoting efficient production;
- liberalizing and stabilizing prices for oilseed production; and,
- promoting competition by increased private participation in certain food industries.

But other self-help provisions have been ignored altogether. They include the goal of reallocating land for domestic food production, along with programs to provide agricultural extension services and education to farmers. Without simultaneous reform redistributing resources toward small farmers and the landless, how could more efficient production benefit them, even if it were to be achieved?

Zaire's record of changes in response to food aid self-help provisions follow suit. The private sector is taking over marketing functions once handled by public agencies, virtually eliminating a role for government in food marketing.[63] Under another provision, a contract system for rice growing is being tested in Zaire's Mongala region. Farmers are to benefit by obtaining "needed manufactured goods," according to AID. As in most such contract arrangements, the firms providing the farmers' supplies retain the exclusive right to buy the farmers' produce at a negotiated price.[64]

Are farmers likely to gain from the new contract system? To the farmer, contract farming often means increased risk and debt, as the Guatemala ALCOSA example highlighted in the preceding chapter. Because the farmer is obligated to sell his rice to the contracting firm, he is in no bargaining position to negotiate a fair price. Plus, the farmer shoulders all of the risk of crop failure.[65] Thus, while contracting may fulfill the nar-

---

63. Ibid., 12–13.

64. Ibid., 14. Specifically, suppliers will have the sole right to purchase the paddy (unprocessed rice) for the first three months of a six-month marketing period.

65. The U.N. Centre on Transnational Corporations implicitly confirms that the farmer takes on more of the risk under contract farming: "Contract farming is less

row goal of stimulating production, experience suggests that the benefits of contract farming go primarily to manufacturers and distributors of farm supplies, and to marketers, not to farmers.[66]

Both Title III and the Gilman-Solarz amendments have the laudable aim of improving the food-producing capabilities of U.S. aid recipients. But the U.S. government cannot be serious about stimulating food production abroad when there is so much pressure to expand exports to get rid of our own agricultural surpluses. In 1986, Congress passed the Bumpers Amendment restricting the funding of projects that might increase or enhance competition with U.S. agricultural exporters. Brazil's soybean production is a classic example of the threat that U.S. producers fear. Although AID was not very involved in promoting Brazil's spectacular growth in soybean exports, the U.S. farm lobby is worried about similar encroachments on other U.S.-dominated markets.[67]

Despite the problems inherent in our food aid program, U.S. food aid promises to increase, not decrease. In mid-1986, *The New York Times* warned that U.S. farmers are now facing

> . . . a grain storage squeeze of historic proportions. . . .
> Nearly every available space in many states . . . will soon
> be overflowing with the bounty of two successive bumper
> harvests.[68]

risky for the foreign investor compared to the direct ownership of plantations." Quoted in Kumar Rupesinghe, "Export Orientation and the Right to Food: The Case of Sri Lanka's Agricultural Promotion Zones," in *Food as a Human Right,* eds. Elde et al., United Nations University, 1984.

66. Under this kind of system, moreover, the contractor is not *obligated* to buy the farmer's output, even though he retains almost complete control over the crops grown and the amount and kind of inputs used. It is not unheard of for contractors to refuse to buy crops whose price has fallen on the world market.

67. IFDP interview, by telephone, with Steve Abrahms, AID Legislative Office, Dec. 10, 1986.

68. William Robbins, "Middle Western Farmers Confront a New Problem: No Storage Space," *The New York Times,* Aug. 4, 1986, A1.

What's to become of these massive stocks of grain? It's quite likely that some will be shipped under P.L. 480, especially if Gramm-Rudman budget cuts reduce the funds available for the U.S. foreign aid program. The temptation will be to replace dollars with food. And some will no doubt make its way overseas under a new food aid category—Section 416, created in the 1981 U.S. Agricultural Act.

Originally designed to dispose of government-owned surplus dairy products, Section 416 was expanded in 1986 to include wheat and wheat products.[69] This new food aid channel currently handles about one-tenth as much in value as the P.L. 480 program.[70] Section 416 commodities are given to foreign governments and to U.S. private organizations to use however they please. Unlike P.L. 480 food aid, Section 416 giveaways are subject to no specific economic development requirements.[71] Even more clearly than its predecessors, therefore, this program can serve as a budgetary support for favored governments. Whether or not it can help the poor depends on the nature of those governments.

The "Humanitarian" Side of Food Aid

When Americans think of food aid as U.S. grain and milk products being handed out directly to hungry children and pregnant women, they're right to the extent that part of it— Title II of P.L. 480—does just that. Because it encompasses a variety of direct feeding programs—including mother-child health projects, food-for-work projects, and emergency relief—Title II is often referred to as the humanitarian side of

---

69. Information from AID P.L. 480 Title I office.

70. Calculated from unpublished AID data contained in "The Exports Under P.L. 480," June 1986.

71. See *The United States Food for Peace Program 1954–84.* International Trade and Development Education Foundation, Spring 1985, 44.

U.S. food aid. Until the Section 416 program, it was the only part of U.S. food aid which was actually given away.

Title II typically makes up about one-third of all U.S. food aid, but its share has risen to as much as one-half during times of severe famine, as in 1985 when large donations of food aid went to Africa.[72] Yet, as a proportion of *all* U.S. government-to-government assistance, Title II is only a drop in the bucket. In the first five years of 1980, only one out of twenty of our aid dollars went to Title II funding.[73]

Most Title II food aid is distributed abroad through large, private American voluntary agencies such as CARE, Catholic Relief Services, Church World Service, or the Seventh Day Adventist international agencies.

Because it is usually given away, Title II food aid is assumed to benefit directly those in need. But many studies—including some funded by AID itself—suggest that food-for-work and direct feeding programs (also known as project food aid) often have little success in reducing malnutrition or in promoting development. Some analysts even go as far as to argue that direct feeding programs are downright harmful to the poor.[74]

Food-for-Work. The idea is very simple: rather than being paid in cash, those who participate in food-for-work schemes get paid with donated food (or some combination of food and cash). Because the wage is invariably low, food-for-work projects become "self-targeting": only the very poorest will work on them.

But who benefits? Some food-for-work projects build roads, with the long-term benefits inevitably going to those wealthy

---

72. *U.S. Overseas Loans and Grants,* various years.

73. Ibid., various years. Total bilateral assistance includes military aid.

74. See Tony Jackson with Deborah Eade, *Against the Grain: The Dilemma of Project Food Aid* (Oxford, U.K.: OXFAM, 1982). It is the best known critique of project food aid, or Title II-type programs. More recently, however, many of the criticisms levied in this book have surfaced in a wealth of Title II evaluations commissioned by AID. (The complete references to these reports are too numerous to list; a bibliographical reference list can be obtained from AID's Office of Program, Policy, and Evaluation.)

enough to have sizable surplus to market (so that road improvements mean easier profits for them). Other projects directly improve the property of the wealthy.[75] In evaluating a U.N. World Food Programme food-for-work project, partially funded with U.S. food donations, the U.N.'s Food and Agriculture Organization (FAO) noted: "[The] project cannot at present refuse any request for assistance even when this request comes from wealthy farmers who ask for the planting and maintenance of several dozen hectares." World Food Programme rations end up paying "the wages of workers employed by large proprietors and gives them the benefits of credits and subsidies intended . . . for the disadvantaged."[76]

Food-for-work projects can take people away from their own food production (willingly or not), critics note, and can increase their dependency on project-supplied food. In the Guatemalan highlands, Indian peasants are building food-for-work roads, primarily for the military, instead of tending their own corn fields.[77] The military has grabbed so much of their land that the Indians are left with little choice but to exchange their labor for food.

In Honduras, an AID official told us that food-for-work was undermining self-help initiatives. "I found that communities which previously were quick to come together to build a local school or clinic would now not do anything unless they were getting food or payment," he lamented.[78] A 1985 AID-sponsored report on food-for-work noted that such programs in

---

75. Though this criticism has been made by many development specialists and aid workers over the years, it was confirmed most recently in a report commissioned by the Bureau of Food for Peace and Voluntary Assistance, part of AID. See John Thomas, "Food For Work—An Analysis of Current Experience and Recommendations," Harvard Institute for International Development, Oct. 1985, 15.

76. Quoted in Jack Shephard, "When Foreign Aid Fails," *The Atlantic Monthly,* Apr. 1985, 44. The U.S. government contributes directly to the World Food program through Title II.

77. Tom Barry, *Guatemala: The Politics of Counterinsurgency* (Albuquerque, N.M.: Inter-Hemispheric Education Resource Center, 1986.)

78. IFDP interview with AID official in Honduras, July 1986.

Haiti and the Dominican Republic "show the futility of trying to substitute food [aid] for the difficult and time-consuming task of building community motivation and cohesion."[79]

Church World Service recently decided to phase out its food-for-work projects in the Caribbean region. According to veteran project officer Peter Graeff, "It took so much time and energy to stop abuses in the program that we never got to do our real development work. When measured against the few benefits of the program, the costs are incredibly high."[80]

Food-for-work could contribute to the local economy if the food to be distributed is locally purchased instead of imported. In Honduras, the German organization, German-Honduran Cooperation Food for Work, buys food within the country which is then used in work projects assisting farm cooperatives and building peasant housing.[81]

Supplementary Feeding Programs. Designed to target those especially vulnerable to malnutrition—young children, and pregnant and lactating women—most supplementary feeding projects are located in schools or health clinics. When children or mothers go to these institutions, they get a ration of free food.

In industrial countries like the United States, such feeding programs may reach the very poor because even the poorest children go to school and many poor people do have access to health clinics. But in the third world, the poorest of the poor cannot afford to go to school or visit a health clinic, so how can feeding programs reach them? Moreover, even when the poorest do receive the food, it does not follow that their total food intake is increased. Children who get supplements at school, for example, may then be given less food at home.

---

79. James M. Pines, et al., *Title II Programs in the Latin America and Caribbean (LAC) Region: Status and Prospects,* a report for the Health and Nutrition Division, LAC/Dr, AID, Oct. 1985, 65.

80. IFDP interview, Port-au-Prince, Haiti, Nov. 1986.

81. IFDP interview, Honduras, Oct. 1986.

Other members of the family might eat slightly more as a result, but the targeted individual has not gained.

Take, for example, the case of a food aid project in the Dominican Republic. Malnourished preschool children were receiving food at a mother-child health center, but other than during the mango and avocado seasons the children gained weight only when the food aid *stopped!* Tony Jackson and Deborah Eade, authors of *Against the Grain: The Dilemma of Project Food Aid* and longtime staff members of OXFAM (U.K.), probed to find out why. They learned that:

> When children received food aid, mothers tended to overestimate the value of this "wonder food" and so fed them less local food. Whenever the food aid failed to arrive, mothers would . . . ensure that their children had food. . . . This resulted in weight gain.[82]

Finally, supplementary feeding programs are not free. While the food itself may be donated, the labor to prepare the food and oversee the operations, overhead expenses, and so on, all add up. Health or teaching personnel may have to take time away from other important activities to help run the program. Even participants pay a price: bringing a child in for a food ration adds to the already heavy demands on a third-world woman. So, while food supplements may provide marginally improved nutrition in some cases, a positive impact cannot simply be assumed. And their costs, both personal and societal, must not be ignored.

Given all of these problems, we have been relieved that several agencies most involved in feeding programs have begun to acknowledge their pitfalls. An official of Catholic Relief Services—which alone distributed $248 million in food in 1985—noted in 1986 that his agency has studied the problems in its feeding programs for years. "We have not been

---

82. Jackson and Eade, *Against the Grain.* 43.

able to demonstrate that our food and nutrition programs have had a uniformly positive impact on the people we are trying to help," he acknowledged.[83]

A 1982 study of supplementary feeding programs prepared for UNICEF was similarly critical, calling the programs' impact "disappointing."[84] The food supplements in most programs were designed to meet about forty to seventy percent of the calorie deficits of the undernourished children, but for the target population as a whole, only ten to twenty-five percent of the calorie gap was closed.

While the negative side-effects of Title II feeding programs may be less severe than those associated with Title I food sales, no one claims that they are a solution to world hunger. As currently constructed, they in no way remove the obstacles—lack of access to land and jobs—that prevent people from being able to provide for themselves. Only in the rare instance that food aid is reconceived as a tool of empowerment can it serve these goals. In Lima, Peru, for example, food aid distributed by the international agency Caritas helped launch poor women toward greater self-sufficiency. The food facilitated the women's efforts to start cooperative kitchens serving many families at once. Cooperative kitchens save fuel; they also save money because the women get discounts by buying in bulk and purchasing food directly from growers. The kitchens save the women time, too, so that they are free to seek other jobs. Complete self-sufficiency is the goal, that is, an end to food aid. The example of successful cooperative kitchens has spurred other women to start up similar group efforts on their own without food aid.

Unfortunately, this example remains exceptional. Because food aid is not structured to address the powerlessness at the

---

83. A CRS official's public statement. (He prefers not to be identified.)

84. George Beaton and Hossein Ghassemi, "Supplementary Feeding Programs for Young Children in Developing Countries," report prepared for UNICEF and the AAC-Subcommittee on Nutrition of the United States, *American Journal of Clinical Nutrition,* 35(4), Apr. 1982, 867.

root of hunger, in most cases it never seems to end. In Bangladesh some sort of food-for-work program has been going on for the last twelve years. Similarly, in the Philippines the Title II program has been operating since 1968, yet hunger in both these nations continues to worsen.[85]

And India, despite the much-heralded Green Revolution success in increasing grain output—generating a thirty million ton grain surplus by 1986—has one of the world's largest Title II feeding programs. In 1984, India, itself a grain exporter, received over one-fifth of all Title II funds, equal to $125.8 million.[86] In that year, almost as many Indians (14.3 million) received U.S. food aid as Americans received food stamps.[87] Yet, as much as half the Indian population does not have enough to eat.[88]

Food Aid: Some Lessons

Nothing could sound more heartless, more Scroogelike, than criticizing food aid, so it is difficult to keep critical facts in focus:

---

85. In both Bangladesh and the Philippines, there can be little doubt that conditions for the poor have deteriorated over the last five to ten years. According to a World Bank report on Bangladesh, for instance, "hardly 5% of the Bangladesh population consumes an adequate quantity or quality of food." (p. 18) Even more importantly, there has been a deterioration in the average intake of calories and protein among the poorest segments of society, "suggesting that the increase in food availability has not been equally distributed among income classes." (Ibid.) (See "Bangladesh: Economic and Social Development Prospects," World Bank Report, no. 5409, Apr. 2, 1985) For references to conditions in the Philippines, see chapter 2.

86. *U.S. Overseas Loans and Grants. July 1, 1945–Sept. 30, 1984.* 4, 15.

87. U.S. Department of Agriculture, Foreign Agricultural Service, *Supplemental Food for Peace: 1984 Annual Report on Public Law 480.* July 1985, table 18.

88. "More Bread, Thinly Sliced," *The Economist.* June 14, 1986, 66. U.S. Department of Agriculture, *World Food Aid Needs and Availabilities* (Washington, D.C.: USDA Economic Research Service, July 1984), table 40.

- Ninety percent of our food aid does not go to emergency famine relief. The bulk is sold by foreign governments to those among their people *who can afford it.*

- Since it is a source of revenue (or frees up other sources) for recipient governments, most food aid must be seen as just another form of budgetary support for favored governments. Like dollar aid, then, it is only as good as the government receiving it. If that government is unaccountable to its people, food aid will largely go toward strengthening the government, not the poor. No number of well-intentioned "strings" attached can change that cruel reality.

- Food can be even more problematic for the poor than economic aid if it undercuts prices that poor farmers need to stay in business. And long-term food security can be made even harder to achieve if food aid contributes to changing tastes toward foods which are difficult to produce locally.

- And finally, since the impetus for U.S. food aid often arises less from the unmet needs of hungry people than from chronic U.S. oversupply problems, surely the United States must reduce its own overproduction before it can have a constructive aid policy. Currently U.S. food aid helps to mask unsolved domestic farm problems, especially overproduction. Here we mean not just surpluses costing millions a year to store, but the overuse of soils, chemical inputs, and groundwater, which jeopardizes the food security of Americans.

The debate on food aid inevitably draws one into a debate of how best to "feed people." But hunger cannot be overcome until people feed themselves. Thus, in the food aid debate lies a danger, the danger of forgetting the obvious: people *will* feed themselves, if they are allowed to do so. This being so, our primary job is to make sure that our tax dollars are not going to strengthen the very forces standing in their way.

A hard, honest look at U.S. food aid reinforces one of the primary themes of our book—that, while profound change in the third world is necessary to allow broad-based development, U.S. aid too often stymies such change. Rethinking our foreign aid with this understanding could lead to efforts to halt chronic U.S. food aid now supporting governments dead set against democratic restructuring. Such a step would not threaten U.S. interests but serve them.

Five

The Free Market and Free Trade: AID's Formula

THE INTENSE DEBATE among aid policymakers over how best to stimulate development in the third world has passed through many phases, as we sketched in chapter 3. But rarely have proponents of a given theory been as cocksure as today's policymakers. President Reagan recently summarized the latest formula:

> We already know what works: private ownership, the freedom to innovate, healthy competition, reliance on market forces, and faith in the strength and inventiveness of the individual citizen. Privatization is premised on all these principles and offers us the surest road to economic renewal for families and nations.[1]

Privatization is the hot new buzz-word. But expanding the private sector while shrinking government is only one aspect in AID's multipronged program for the third world. In addition, AID's formula for development includes expanding

---

1. Quoted in "Privatization and the Private Sector: Keys to Third World Development," *AID Highlights,* vol. 3, no. 2, Summer 1986, 1.

trade and luring foreign investment. To attract that investment, AID recommends removing disincentives: corporate
taxes, uncompetitive wages, and regulations that might inter-
fere with U.S. corporations making—and taking out of a country—large profits.[2]

All of these steps will stimulate economic growth, Washington tells the third world. And as we stressed—and chal-
lenged—in chapter 3, growth to U.S. policymakers is
synonymous with development.

AID's love affair with the private sector is not new. Ever
since the post-World War II Marshall Plan invested billions of
dollars in strengthening the business classes of Western
Europe,[3] U.S. foreign aid has sought to foster private enterprise. The Alliance for Progress under President John F.
Kennedy was designed to bolster the business sector in Latin
America and link it to the U.S. economy. Kennedy proudly
pointed to "our increased efforts to encourage the investment
of private capital in the underdeveloped countries."[4]

Even as the programmatic emphasis shifted to basic human

---

2. AID's use of conditionality to achieve macroeconomic policy reforms is not
entirely new. In the early 1960s, AID conditioned its assistance to Brazil, Chile, India,
Korea, and Turkey, among other countries, on the adoption of a number of policy
changes. Beginning in the early 1970s, however, the use of conditionality tapered off
with the advent of the New Directions legislation. The Reagan administration has
revived and expanded the policy of placing conditions on U.S. foreign assistance. For
a discussion of four such programs (in Jamaica, Liberia, Costa Rica, and the Dominican Republic), see: U.S. Government Accounting Office, *U.S. Use of Conditions to
Achieve Economic Reforms,* report no. GAO/NSIAD-86-157 (Washington, D.C.: U.S.
GAO, Aug. 1986).

3. Most Americans have been taught that the Marshall Plan was about "rebuilding
Europe." But the goal was narrower—it was to revitalize the discredited business
classes. During World War II many European business leaders either fled with as
much wealth as they could, were killed and/or had their assets destroyed, or col-
laborated with fascism, which lowered their credibility in the postwar political arena.
The most serious opposition to the Nazis came from socialists and communists. So,
in the immediate postwar period, a key objective of U.S. leaders was to strengthen
the business classes to enable them to regain control of the political process in their
respective countries. (Joyce and Gabriel Kolko, *The Limits of Power: The World and
United States Foreign Policy 1945 to 1954* [New York: Harper and Row, 1972], chapters
13, 16.)

4. Cited in Emilio Collado, "Economic Development Through Private Enterprise," *Foreign Affairs,* July 1963, 715.

needs in the 1970s, considerable funds went to infrastructure—energy, transportation, irrigation—built by private contractors and benefiting primarily local business groups and larger farmers.[5] And throughout the postwar period, one private sector has been a consistent beneficiary of U.S. foreign aid—the U.S. corporate sector. As noted earlier, seventy percent of all aid dollars sent abroad have consistently been spent on goods and services produced by U.S. firms.[6]

What is new about the 1980s is the Reagan administration's exclusive emphasis on the role of business, infusing the private enterprise thrust with more funds and the conviction of a true believer.

Less Government, More Progress?

It's assumed that private investment equals growth and measurable economic return, while public investment saps an economy's vigor. Yet a 1985 World Bank report on the economic return on investments in education offers striking counterevidence. It shows that the rate of return on human investments—health, and education, for example—is higher than on capital investments. "In developing countries . . . there is a clear advantage of human versus physical capital investment," it concludes.[7] Yet such investments in "human capital" are precisely what private wealth neglects because it can't capture the full return, which accrues not only to the individual but to society as a whole.

The goal of current policy is not merely to shift investment

5. See Institute for Food and Development Policy, *Aid As Obstacle: Twenty Questions About Our Foreign Aid and the Hungry* (San Francisco: Food First Books, 1981).

6. "Private Enterprise: The Key to Development," *AID Highlights,* vol. 1, no. 2, Summer 1984, 4.

7. George Psacharopoulos, "Return to Education: A Further International Update and Implications," World Bank Reprint Series, no. 362, 590–591. Originally in *The Journal of Human Resources,* vol. 20, no. 4, Fall 1985.

funds toward the private sector, however; it is to expand the private sector by trimming government's role.

FOR SALE: GOVERNMENT ENTERPRISES

Arguing that many economic activities can be performed more efficiently by private companies than by governments, AID urges that state corporations should be turned over to the private sector.

In many countries, increasing the efficiency of government operations is not only reasonable—it is necessary. But a key defect in AID's reasoning is that efficiency is defined strictly in financial terms.[8] A government may save money by privatizing state corporations and laying off workers, but the savings may be lost after adding in hidden social costs. The poor and even the middle class may suffer from the cutbacks in services and employment that result because the private sector simply does not take up what government has dropped. As an AID official in the Dominican Republic admitted to us: "the private sector can't possibly create the amount of jobs needed."[9]

Honduras is just one country where AID has been pushing the government to sell state enterprises to the private sector. Gautama Fonseca, former Minister of Labor, exposes the simplemindedness of assuming that such a shift will automatically bring economic improvement.

> This idea of privatization is nutty. They're touting it as if they've discovered something new. What do they think has been the predominant system here for the past century? How do they think we got in this mess to begin with?
>
> There is nothing more inefficient and corrupt in Honduras than private enterprise. They steal millions of dol-

---

8. AID's privatization argument reinforces the view that all state enterprises are inefficient, when, in fact, some government agencies (e.g., Zimbabwe's Grain Marketing Board) are quite efficient.

9. IFDP interview, Santo Domingo, Dominican Republic, Nov. 1986.

lars every year from the government, from the people. Now we're supposed to sell off our public enterprises at rock-bottom prices to the thieves and mafiosos who sucked the government corporations dry to begin with.[10]

An African might make a similar retort to U.S. advice to governments there to sell state marketing boards to private interests. These boards—government agencies with exclusive rights to market key crops—were created in many African countries in colonial times. Their purpose was to facilitate extraction of wealth from the countryside for enrichment of the colonizing country and to ensure the profits of rich farmers, especially white settlers. They are equally destructive today where wealthy farmers are a powerful political force. "Large producers are favored over small producers" by the boards, and "exports are favored over domestic production. The inefficiencies of the marketing boards and the high transport charges also fall disproportionately upon the smallholder," one study of Kenya concludes.[11]

But simply selling these government bodies to the private sector is not likely to help the majority of small farmers. The same study critical of the state boards also notes the poor record of private institutions, such as commercial banks. They, too, favor the wealthy farmers.[12]

In Senegal, AID, along with the IMF and the World Bank, has pushed the government to sell several of its development agencies. One is SAED (Société d'Aménagement Economique des Terres du Delta), the agency responsible for irrigation and development of the critically important Senegal River Basin. Although not completely dismantled, SAED's

---

10. IFDP interview, Tegucigalpa, Honduras, July 1986.

11. Stephen Peterson, "Neglecting the Poor: State Policy Toward the Smallholder in Kenya," in Stephen K. Commins, Michael F. Lofchie, and Rhys Payne, *Africa's Agrarian Crisis: The Roots of Famine* (Boulder, Col.: Lynne Rienner, 1986), 72.

12. Ibid., 74.

role in the provision of irrigation has been greatly scaled back.[13]

Senegalese peasants may end up worse off than before, according to John Sutter, an agricultural project officer for the Ford Foundation. "If agribusiness wins control over irrigation, it will probably try to take over the peasants' lands and force them to become wage laborers."[14] The Senegalese peasant farmer will be completely cut out of the decision-making process if the corporate private sector takes over.

> Even though SAED may be inefficient and top-down, at least it involved the farmer in its irrigation decisions. Once outside private traders and moneylenders get involved, it's not clear that farmers will even be consulted about what irrigation facilities they want or need.[15]

Moreover, the push to sell off government agencies includes no planning for reemployment of government workers. Cutbacks in SAED and other government rural development agencies in Senegal led to the firing of 1,500 government workers.[16] Reducing the number of government officials might well be justified, but to achieve development goals, this cutback must go hand in hand with plans for alternative employment.

AID's formulistic approach ignores critical questions:

- Might government marketing make sense in certain crops? Could *both* government and private marketing have a useful role to play? Might competition between the two make each more efficient?

- In more remote areas which private firms might neglect, would a public agency in marketing or irrigation

---

13. SAED still provides extension services to farmers.

14. IFDP interview with John Sutter, Feb. 2, 1986, Berkeley, Calif.

15. Ibid.

16. U.S. Agency for International Development, *Congressional Presentation. Fiscal Year 1987.* Africa vol., 360.

be needed? Might a public agency be the only vehicle to insure that private institutions, such as the banks mentioned above, serve the smaller farmers as well as the bigger ones?

• How could a government agency be more effectively organized for productivity and equity?

AID's simplistic belief that the answer lies in ending the government's role in the economy ignores the history of industrial capitalist countries like the United States, England, and Japan. They achieved their current levels of development with extensive government intervention in markets. Similarly, AID ignores lessons from third-world countries that have enjoyed rapid economic growth—countries as different as South Korea, Taiwan, and Brazil—where governments have intervened heavily in the economy.

"PRIVATE" DOESN'T EQUAL "CORPORATE"

Finally, converting a state enterprise into a private one need not mean selling it to a large private corporation. The state could also sell the operation to the workers, which is what the British government did in the early 1980s with the country's largest trucking firm, the National Freight Corporation. Productivity increased thirty percent and the value of each share of stock rose one thousand percent, making many of the employees quite wealthy.[17] Some privatization specialists argue that such "employee takeover or buy-out" is "more applicable to LDCs [less developed countries] than conventional privatization."[18] Yet in its promotional efforts, the U.S. government ignores this more democratic form of privatization.

---

17. Cited in Dr. Madsen Pirie and Peter Young, "Public and Private Responsibilities in Privatization," paper presented to International Conference on Privatization, sponsored by AID, Feb. 17–19, 1986, 9.

18. Ibid.

In arguing "private is good, public is bad," the free market advocates create a false dichotomy. Economic systems involve many actors—trade unions, cooperatives, self-help groups, and other intermediate organizations—which are neither government bodies nor private corporations. Indeed, our research has found that the most dynamic forces for progress in the third world are precisely these citizens' groups which don't fit into the artificial dichotomy of public vs. private.[19] Most important, posing the development problem in terms of this dichotomy obscures the crucial question of democratic control. Within the private sector is the small farmer as well as the large, hierarchical corporation; and governments range from popular to dictatorial. The question is less which sector controls a given economic activity than the extent to which average citizens are empowered in directing the activity.

Reducing Government Deficits

Even after piling up more federal debt than all previous U.S. administrations combined, the Reagan administration has no compunction about advising other nations how to reduce theirs. To the many governments consistently spending more money than they take in, AID has the answer: cut expenditures, such as government food subsidies, and charge fees for using government services, including health care and education.

In Jamaica, the government's efforts to "rationalize" the hospital system by closing smaller clinics has forced sick people to travel greater distances to the larger, regional hospitals. The medical officer in charge of Kingston, the capital, told us

19. See our discussion of such groups in the final pages of chapter 3. For a fuller discussion, see the special issues of the following magazines which our Institute co-produced: *The Food Monitor,* no. 36, Spring 1986 and *Seeds,* vol. 9, no. 8, Aug. 1986.

that the cutbacks have saved money, but at a human cost. Sick people in rural areas where a local clinic has shut down often can't make the trek to a regional hospital. Laying off and cutting pay to doctors, nurses, and other staff have exacerbated brain-drain, as professionals migrate to the United States in search of higher salaries. The result is a marked decline of Jamaica's health care system.

KEEPING FOOD CHEAP

Dozens of governments have some type of food subsidy program. They range from food stamps and supplementary feeding programs for pregnant women, infants, and the elderly, to more all-encompassing programs such as food rationing, where limited amounts of critical commodities are distributed to every family at low prices, and "fair price shops," where limited amounts of food are sold below market prices.

Food subsidy programs can improve the nutrition of millions of people and raise the purchasing power of the poor. In Kerala, India, for example, effective subsidies for food and other essential items are linked to lower infant death rates and impressive longevity, compared to other states in India. The subsidies account for as much as one-fifth of the income of Kerala's poorer families.[20] From the early 1950s onward, health and welfare in Sri Lanka have been improved in large part due to the government's provision, until 1978, of highly subsidized rice.[21] (After the late seventies, Sri Lanka moved toward the export industrialization, "free market" model now promoted by Washington, and cut its food program.)

But food subsidies can also be used by governments as political patronage, with many of the benefits going to middle class consumers, civil servants, and the military.

---

20. A. V. Jose, "Poverty and Inequality—the Case of Kerala," in *Poverty in Rural Asia,* Azizur Rahman Khan and Eddy Lee, eds. (Bangkok: International Labour Organization, Asian Employment Programme, 1983), 107ff.

21. *Sri Lanka: The Impact of P.L. 480 Title I Food Assistance* AID Project Impact Evaluation Report, no. 39, Oct. 1982, especially app. F.

Food subsidies are tricky to manage without negative side-effects. Governments trying to keep food prices down will also be tempted to pay low prices to farmers, undercutting their incentives to grow more food. But if governments assure the farmer a decent price while subsidizing retail food prices, the difference between what the government pays farmers and what it receives from consumers can get out of hand. Roughly one-third of Egypt's national budget is soaked up by subsidies for basic necessities, especially bread.[22]

Despite these problems, many governments—rightly—view food subsidies as essential to their very survival. In many third-world countries poor people pay three-fourths or more of their income for food, so even subsidized prices don't mean cheap food to them. Where many people live at the edge of survival, food prices shooting out of reach due to cuts in government subsidies have brought on riots and the downfall of more than one government.[23]

In Egypt in 1977, dozens of people were shot dead by government forces during protests over reduced food subsidies. Liberia's rice riots of 1979 helped to spark the ouster of the Tolbert regime. In 1984, Tunisia cut subsidies, leading to an overnight doubling of the price of bread. Resulting riots left eighty-nine people dead.

Understandably, some of the rioters' rage is directed at the United States. Imagine a foreign government telling the United States to cut its food stamp program and then providing guns and tear gas to repress Americans when they protested the cutbacks.

Food subsidies are not the answer to a country's food problems. They are a palliative that leaves intact the underlying problem—the lack of sufficient purchasing power to buy even such a primary necessity as food. To make food subsidies unnecessary would involve nothing less than far-reaching eco-

---

22. John Kifner, "The Egyptian Economy Has No Place to Turn," *The New York Times*, July 6, 1986.

23. David K. Willis, "Link Between Aid Terms and Riots in Africa," *Christian Science Monitor*, Apr. 16, 1985, 1.

nomic reform redistributing access to the society's resources. Until full employment, land reform, and other changes allow people to afford full prices for food, government food subsidies for the poor will be essential to their survival. No magic of the marketplace will change this basic fact.

THE OTHER SIDE OF THE LEDGER

AID's prescription for reducing government deficits leaves out one side of the ledger. A deficit can be reduced by increasing revenues as effectively as by reducing expenditures. In most third-world countries the tax system is notoriously ineffective and frequently unfair. Many of the very wealthy pay virtually nothing.[24]

When AID does propose changes in a country's tax system, it usually recommends reducing taxes on the wealthy to encourage them to invest. AID's Country Development Strategy Statement for the Dominican Republic, for example, complains about "the 18 percent tax and 3 percent surtax on profit repatriation from foreign investments."[25]

> These taxes and surcharges create uncertainty in the business community, contribute to a lack of confidence in equitable government administration, cause economic distortions, and deter foreign investment. . . . Legislation is needed to remove the taxes and surtaxes.[26]

Thus, at the same time that AID advises third-world governments to reduce government deficits, they are telling these

---

24. In Haiti, for example, following decades of the U.S.-backed Duvalier dictatorship, there were only 1,762 registered taxpayers in a population of 5 million. (*Haiti Times,* Oct. 1986, 1). Yet in Jan. 1985, under prompting from the U.S. government, the Haitian government adopted a new investment code which provides extensive tax exemptions and 100 percent repatriation of profits. (Ibid., 7).

25. AID, *Dominican Republic Country Development Strategy Statement, FY 1987,* Jan. 28, 1986, 8.

26. Ibid., 8–9.

same governments to offer generous tax *breaks* to foreign corporations in order to lure investment.

In its unwillingness to consider both sides of the government ledger equally, AID reveals its bias in favor of status quo inequities in the distribution of wealth and income.

Luring Private Investment

To spur private investment—both local and foreign—AID advises governments to lower taxes, hold down wages, and loosen restrictions on taking profits out of the country. When businessmen are assured of a good profit, goes the theory, they will invest and thereby contribute to the development of the country.

Even if successful, attracting foreign investment is not necessarily the answer to development problems in the eyes of all third-world leaders. Selling public agencies could attract foreign investment, but some see it merely deepening a relationship of dependency. Former Honduran Labor Minister Guatama Fonseca asked us in a recent interview:

> Who has the money to buy these giant enterprises? Most Hondurans are impoverished. The only ones with enough money are the *gringos;* so privatization means selling our country, bit by bit, to foreigners. It means becoming a colony of the United States. It's worse than in the beginning of the century when we sold our land to the banana companies.[27]

A Haitian businessman with whom we spoke echoes Fonseca's fears. "The Haitian businessmen like the sound of privatization because they think they are going to get to buy these companies cheap," he told us. "But no bank here is going to let Haitian businessmen outbid the foreigners. The U.S. pri-

---

27. IFDP interview, Tegucigalpa, Honduras, July 1986.

vate sector will swallow up the Haitian private sector because they don't need us."[28]

But even if one were to accept AID's goal of increased private investment as the place to start, two problems remain.

First, how is development-stimulating investment possible without essential activities—building and maintaining roads, railways, electric grids, and water supplies, for example—which are rarely undertaken by private enterprise? Most are not profitable from the point of view of a single firm; they are only profitable from the point of view of the entire society. Such vital tasks are among the primary functions of government. But AID's current fixation on the private sector ignores this critical aspect of development necessary to get its own private investment program off the ground.

Second, how can AID's plan succeed in luring private investment if the ingredients for profit making just aren't there? Take Sub-Saharan Africa. Most Africans are too poor to constitute an attractive market, so the only kind of investors the region might attract are those interested in extraction of raw materials or production for export. Add to this the lack of infrastructure, the depletion of Africa's natural resources, and the massive foreign debt that is bankrupting many African states, and it becomes clear why capital is not just failing to come into the region, it is *deserting.* "In 1980, African countries got close to $1.5 billion, net, from private creditors; in 1985 there was a net outflow of $700 million," reports *The Economist.* [29]

Africa is the worst case, but it is not alone. Overall, net direct investment in third-world economies is falling. In 1983 it was $2.4 billion, forty percent below levels of just two years earlier.[30]

---

28. IFDP interview with Robert Duval, member of the Manufacturer's Association of Port-au-Prince, Nov. 1986.

29. "How Much Africa Needs," *The Economist,* June 7, 1986, 81.

30. Richard E. Feinberg, "International Finance and Investment: A Surging Public Sector," in John Sewell et al., eds., *U.S. Foreign Policy and the Third World: Agenda*

Not only are the conditions to attract foreign investment often absent, but local wealth is also rapidly exiting. In the Philippines under Ferdinand Marcos, some foreign businessmen were attracted by the "labor peace" martial law created. But capital flight was so widespread—Marcos and his cronies alone are estimated to have spirited away some $20 billion—that the country was left hovering on the edge of bankruptcy when he fled.[31] "Every year, billions of dollars flow out of Brazil and much of Latin America . . . much of it in violation of local currency laws," reports the *The New York Times*.[32] When we asked a U.S. Embassy official in Honduras where all the U.S. economic aid to that country was going, he groaned: "most of it ends up in private bank accounts in Miami."[33]

The lesson is clear: if a lucrative market does not exist locally, foreign firms will not be eager to invest, except to produce for export. Nor will local firms and wealthy individuals reinvest their earnings locally if more lucrative investments exist overseas. Within AID's formula, this problem has no solution. Its free enterprise dogma opposes government controls to keep profits at home. How then can governments even keep existing capital from fleeing, much less attract new capital?

Faced with a heavy foreign debt and a desperate need for development capital, in 1986 the President of Peru, Alan Garcia, tried to deal with the problem by suspending repatriation of all profits by foreign corporations, and limiting interest payments on the national debt.[34] This is precisely the kind of action which would put a country on Washington's blacklist.

1985–86. U.S.-Third World Policy Perspective, no. 3, Overseas Development Council, (New Brunswick, N.J.: Transaction Books, 1985), 65.

31. "Marcos and the Election Mess," *Newsweek*, Feb. 17, 1986, 18.

32. Marlise Simons, "Focus on Latin Flight of Capital," *The New York Times*, May 27, 1986, 25.

33. IFDP interview, Tegucigalpa, Sept. 1984.

34. "Peru Takes the Lead," *Gatt-Fly Report*, vol. 7, no. 4, Nov. 1986, 5. (Published by GATT-Fly, 11 Madison Ave., Toronto, Ontario Canada M5R2S2.)

AID believes that it can overcome this central constraint on profitability—the widespread poverty of the majority—by special incentives to make business profitable anyway. AID launched a program in 1982 called the Private Enterprise Initiative to give support to business ventures in the third world. In the Caribbean, for example, AID provides funds to pay for U.S. business advisers to help identify business opportunities, to construct factory infrastructure, and to revitalize businessmen's organizations. AID's prohibition against government involvement apparently operates when dealing with government restrictions on business, but rarely with government *boosts* to business.

Are More Exports the Answer?

DEVALUATION AND DEVELOPMENT

For the many third-world countries suffering from balance of trade deficits—spending more on imported goods and services than is earned from exports—AID prescribes devaluing local currencies. By making the country's products more affordable in foreign currencies, devaluation will increase the volume of exports, goes the theory. Foreign customers will increase their purchases more than enough to compensate for what is lost to the exporter in lower prices per unit.

But this neat solution misses essential pieces in the export/import puzzle. First, *devaluation also makes imports more expensive.* If a country's exports are produced largely with imported components and machinery, how can it be assured of a net gain even if exports increase?

Jamaica's economy illustrates the problem. Nearly half of the supplies and equipment used in Jamaican manufacturing are imported. Thus, devaluing the Jamaican dollar in the early 1980s—making imports more expensive—sent production costs soaring. Many exporters of manufactured goods were forced to cut back production or shut down entirely. Even the Jamaican Manufacturers' Association, once a staunch supporter of conservative Prime Minister Edward Seaga, criticized the shortsightedness of the reform.[35]

Consumer imports—everything from corn flakes to toothpaste—also became more expensive as a result of devaluation. Consequences were devastating for most Jamaicans who had already suffered from cuts in subsidies on food, transportation, and utilities. Prices of many essential items doubled and tripled by 1983.[36] During a 1986 research trip, a typical working class mother told us: "I'm so ashamed, I can't even afford to send my children to school anymore."[37] Even AID admits that "rising prices have eroded the real purchasing power of Jamaicans whose incomes have not kept pace with cost-of-living increases."[38]

Second, devaluation as the key to increasing exports overlooks the fact that important third-world exports such as sugar, meat, or textiles face restricted access to the largest market— the United States—due to U.S. government import quotas. These quotas assign a given share of the U.S. market to each allied country exporting a particular product. Given the quota system, lowering the price via devaluation will not necessarily expand these sales. Many other countries in Europe and Japan also have similar restrictions on third-world exports.

Third, the assumption that cheaper third-world commodities will automatically expand sales runs up against the reality of saturated markets in the industrial countries. Foreign con-

---

35. Paul Thomas, President, Jamaican Manufacturers' Association, "Structural Adjustment and the Jamaican Manufacturing Sector: 1982–1985," paper for symposium on "Deregulation and the Jamaican Economy," University of West Indies, Mona, Nov. 30, 1985.

36. *Washington Post National Weekly Edition,* Feb. 11, 1984, 19.

37. IFDP interview, Jan. 1986, Kingston, Jamaica.

38. AID, *Congressional Presentation, FY 1986,* Latin America and Caribbean, vol. 1, 89.

sumers will not rush out to buy more bananas just because the price falls a few cents. Thus government and business leaders in a country like Honduras aren't being stubborn when they resist U.S. pressure to devalue the *lempira*. They know that devaluation would leave their banana exporters selling roughly the same quantity but at lower prices.

Fourth, an AID officer in the Caribbean reminded us that there's nothing in AID's plan to prevent recipient governments from trying to compete against one another by ever steeper devaluations, ultimately cutting all throats.

Finally, devaluation of a third-world currency makes it cheaper for foreign corporations to do what Fonseca and the Haitian businessman we quoted above most fear: buy up the land and successful local companies. In the Dominican Republic, for example, devaluation of the peso has allowed U.S. corporations to buy fertile farmland and turn it into high-priced tourist resorts.

COMPARATIVE ADVANTAGE RECONSIDERED

The renewed emphasis on exports is a revival of the old comparative advantage trade theory. Applied to agriculture, the theory holds that each country should export whatever brings the highest profit in international trade, even if that means exporting specialty crops and importing essential foodstuffs.

But what sounds commonsensical in theory can lock economies onto a dangerous track. While it may be cheaper for some countries to import staple foods today, this is largely because current U.S. and European agricultural policies have generated enormous oversupplies of grain which they are willing to sell at highly subsidized prices. What would happen if these policies were to change radically in the future—as may occur, due to their continually rising cost to the exporting countries' governments? Many third-world nations could not pay a larger food import bill.

Africa's experience during the 1970s underscores the problem. While the volume of Africa's cereal imports tripled over the decade, costs rose over twice as fast—a staggering 600 percent.[39] And what is the future for a country like Belize—which AID touts as a "natural greenhouse, capable of providing the U.S. with fresh winter fruits and vegetables"—if it already spends one-quarter of its GNP on imported food?[40]

In *World Hunger: Twelve Myths,* we explore other fallacies in the notion that greater exports alone can stimulate broad-based development.[41] The claim that third-world countries have a comparative advantage, for example, in exports of labor-intensive electronic goods because their labor is so cheap, fails to point out the implication: that the only way such an economy can continue to compete is for workers to remain underpaid. Their "development" hinges, then, on their continued poverty—isn't the contradiction all too obvious?

The core of the theory, however, assumes the foreign exchange earned by exports will be invested in long-term development needs. But this can't be assumed in countries where national priorities put the importation of luxury goods, weapons, or materials to build showcase projects like hotels and airports above the basic needs of the people. In one typical example: Mexico's export earnings shot up a spectacular twelvefold during the 1970s while the portion used to import food fell from twelve to nine percent. The absolute amount of imported food increased dramatically, *but* four-fifths were luxury foods—meat, feed grains, and alcoholic beverages available only to the better off.[42]

39. Office of Technology Assessment, *Africa Tomorrow: Issues in Technology, Agriculture and U.S. Foreign Aid* (Washington, D.C., United States Government Printing Office, Dec. 1984), 19.

40. Judy Van Rest, "Partners in Development: Belize," *AID Horizons,* Spring 1986, 15.

41. Frances Moore Lappé and Joseph Collins, *World Hunger: Twelve Myths* (New York and San Francisco: Grove Press/Food First Books, 1986), chapter 8.

42. Calculated from World Bank, *World Tables 1983,* tables 2 and 6. Food and Agriculture Organization, *FAO Trade Yearbook 1983,* vol. 37 (Rome: FAO, 1984); and Food and Agriculture Organization, *FAO Trade Yearbook 1975,* vol. 29 (Rome: FAO, 1976).

THE CARIBBEAN BASIN INITIATIVE:
"A NICE IDEA"

Following the 1979 revolutions in Grenada and Nicaragua, U.S. policymakers decided to take preventive measures to stave off such developments elsewhere. The theory of comparative advantage helped shape their response in the form of the Caribbean Basin Initiative (CBI). The CBI was launched in 1983 to stimulate economic growth and job creation by strengthening businesses in the economically stagnant Caribbean Basin. The primary stated goal of the initiative is to stimulate these countries' exports to the United States.

The CBI provides for twelve years of duty-free access for certain commodities to U.S. markets. In return, the United States asks participating governments to devalue their currencies, eliminate tariffs, and "change policies that artificially overprice labor"[43]—policies, that is, which improve wages and benefits.

But three years into the program, the World Bank concluded that the CBI's "trade provisions have had negligible effects so far."[44] No doubt part of the reason is that eighty-seven percent of Caribbean exports were *already* entering the United States duty-free due to pre-CBI trade preferences.[45]

More important, what the United States offers with one hand to the Caribbean nations, it takes away with the other. Since 1982, at the behest of the U.S. sugar growers' lobby,[46] Washington has repeatedly cut the quota for sugar imports from the region, reducing the Caribbean sugar producers'

---

43. AID, *Congressional Presentation, FY 1986,* Latin America and the Caribbean, annex III, vol. 1, 20.

44. World Bank, *World Development Report 1986* (Washington, D.C.: World Bank, 1986), 144.

45. Tom Barry, Beth Wood, and Deb Preusch, *The Other Side of Paradise: Foreign Control in the Caribbean* (New York: Grove Press, 1984), 164.

46. Another important force lobbying for restrictions on U.S. sugar imports were the U.S. corn farmers whose product—corn syrup sweetener—now accounts for forty-five percent of the U.S. sweetener market and would be hurt by competition from Caribbean sugar.

export earnings by $300 million between 1984 and 1986.[47]

Then, to make amends for the damage wrought by reducing the sugar quota, the United States offered the Caribbean countries grants of rice, soybeans, and wheat. Instead of helping, such largesse only compounded the damage. Sugar producers trying to diversify into other crops found their prices undercut by free U.S. food flooding the markets. "It gets to be comical," State Department official Richard Holwill comments. "It makes us look like damn fools when we go down there and preach free enterprise."[48]

Though the CBI may not be a boon to Caribbean exports, it *has* helped some American corporations that export. According to the loan agreements which qualify a country for the CBI, any part of the funds used for imports must be spent on U.S. goods and services—*even if they might be found cheaper elsewhere.*[49] Also, the type of investments being made under the CBI are heavily import dependent, relying on U.S. technologies, raw materials, and services.[50]

A few U.S. corporations may benefit, but Caribbean businessmen doubt that their firms are gaining from the CBI. Caribbean governments "are so busy wooing foreign investors that the needs of local manufacturers are being ignored," concludes the Development Group for Alternative Policies.[51] A 1986 survey conducted by the five major business associations in Haiti found that nearly three-fourths of the companies responding to the survey felt the program had "not really" helped them or had helped "not at all."[52]

"The Caribbean Basin Initiative was a nice idea," con-

---

47. Clifford Krauss, "U.S. Sugar Quotas Impede U.S. Policies Toward Latin America," *The Wall Street Journal,* Sept. 26, 1986.

48. Quoted in Ibid.

49. Barry, Wood, and Preusch, *The Other Side of Paradise,* 165.

50. Atherton Martin, Steve Hellinger and David Solomon, "Prospects and Reality: The CBI Revisited," report by the Development Group for Alternative Policies, Inc., 26.

51. Ibid., 27.

52. "Alliance Secteur Prive Releases Survey Results," *Haiti Times,* Oct. 1986, 9.

cluded *The Washington Post,* but "limited trade concessions are
not a very powerful force for small countries' development in
a time in which the world economy is expanding only slowly,
commodity prices are falling and protectionism is on the
rise."[53] By late 1986, three years after the CBI's launching,
Caribbean exports to the United States were earning fewer
dollars than when the CBI was initiated.[54]

GOOD MEDICINE FOR THEM, NOT FOR US

Preaching the wonders of the market, U.S. policymakers
might well look like "damn fools," as the State Department's
spokesman put it. For Washington hardly follows its own advice.

According to the World Bank, "the industrial countries
have erected high barriers to imports of temperate-zone products from developing countries and then have subsidized
their own exports."[55] The industrial nations also place what
are called nontariff trade barriers on about twenty percent of
all imports from the third world. Yet nontariff barriers cover
only ten percent of trade among the industrial countries themselves.[56] Not surprisingly, the World Bank concludes that
"the special trade preference schemes [that the industrial na-
tions] have extended to many developing countries have not
been a significant offset to their trade restrictions."[57]

Moreover, the type of trade barriers maintained by Western
governments pose a special handicap: they enforce third-
world countries' dependence on raw material exports, blocking further industrialization. Industrial countries' "tariffs are
higher on more highly processed forms of a good," reports

---

53. "In the Caribbean," *The Washington Post Weekly Edition.* Nov. 17, 1986, 26.

54. Ibid.

55. World Bank, *World Development Report 1986* (Washington, D.C.: World Bank, 1986), 11.

56. Ibid., 40.

57. Ibid., 11.

the World Bank. "As goods become more highly processed—and embody more labor and capital services—developing countries face increasing barriers to sales in the world's major markets."[58]

AID'S EXPORT DEAD-END

AID's reasoning behind its emphasis on export-led growth is simple: for private enterprise to be successful, it must have a market. And because most people in the third world are too poor to buy the goods their own countries produce, production for export is the only profitable strategy. But because AID's strategy does nothing to address what created the problem in the first place—vast economic inequality—it is ultimately doomed to defeat itself. As we have seen, wealth will continue to leave, undermining the possibility for self-sustaining development.

AID's export-oriented strategy also exposes third-world economies to world market forces over which they have no control. For third-world exporters, this has meant the decline in prices for their commodities and the rise in prices for the manufactured goods they import. All major categories of third-world exports suffered real price declines during the post-World War II period.[59] In contrast to price declines of raw materials, prices of manufactured exports from industrial

---

58. Ibid., 126.

59. *Real Growth of Commodity prices,* 1950–1984

COMMODITY	AVERAGE ANNUAL PERCENT CHANGE
Total agriculture	−1.03
Beverages	−1.13
Cereals	−1.30
Fats and oils	−1.29
Raw materials	−1.08
Metals and minerals	−0.09

Source: World Bank, *World Development Report 1986* (Washington, D.C.: World Bank, 1986), 7.

countries averaged annual real *increases* of 5.4 percent during 1965–73 and 11 percent during 1973–80.[60]

With declining prices, a country can have great "success" in increasing exports—with virtually no gain in revenue. Argentina, for example, upped the volume of its agricultural exports by almost fifty percent between 1980 and 1985, while revenues from such exports rose a mere *three* percent![61]

No hope of price recovery is in sight for third-world exporters, according to business analyst Peter Drucker. Synthetics and new industrial processes are today replacing many third-world raw material exports.[62] Communications equipment that previously required tons of copper wire, now requires only pounds of glass fiber optics; fields of sugar cane cannot compete with factory-produced Nutrasweet and corn syrup sweetener from the North American farm belt.

The vicious cycle of debt and rising interest payments bankrupting many third-world nations today is in part a result of their borrowing from Western banks in an attempt to fill the gap between rising import costs and falling export revenues.

Models of Success?

The Sri Lankan government has earned kudos from AID because it has "shifted away from public sector domination . . . and prospered from creating a more attractive climate for private enterprise."[63] It's worth examining the lessons that Sri Lanka has to teach.

---

60. Ibid., 25.

61. Joint Economic Committee of Congress, "The Impact of the Latin American Debt Crisis on the U.S. Economy," May 1986.

62. Peter Drucker, "The Changed World Economy," *Foreign Affairs*, Spring 1986, 771, 774–775. As the World Bank reported in 1986, "The decline in the price of primary commodities relative to the price of manufactures also reflects an underlying trend toward more efficient use of materials and increased substitution of synthetics." *World Development Report 1986*, 37.

63. "Private Enterprise: The Key to Economic Development," *AID Highlights*, vol. 1, no. 2, Summer 1984.

In 1977, a new political party took office, bringing sweeping changes in the country's economy. It reversed the previous policies of tightly regulated foreign investment and external trade, opened Sri Lanka's doors to foreign capital, and embraced an export orientation.[64] At the same time that the Sri Lankan government decided to liberalize its economy, it began dismantling the social safety net which had made Sri Lanka a leader among poor countries in life expectancy, infant survival, and nutrition.

Such changes led to a doubling of the economic growth rate from three to six percent since 1977, but mounting evidence suggests that this growth has not benefited the rich and poor equally.[65] In fact, one of AID's own evaluations notes that the distribution of income worsened in Sri Lanka between the early and late 1970s, due in part to the "economic liberalization program initiated by the new government."[66] Another AID-sponsored evaluation reported in dry understatement: "Not all Sri Lankan households were equally well-positioned

---

64. For more detail of Sri Lanka's economic reforms, see H. N. S. Karunatilake, "The Impact of Sri Lanka's Economic Reforms in 1977 on Employment and Income Distribution," *The Philippine Review of Economics and Business,* vol. 19, 1982, 281–295; and, Kumar Rupesinghe, "Export Orientation and the Right to Food: The Case of Sri Lanka's Agricultural Export Zones" in Asbjorn Elde, et al., eds., *Food as a Human Right,* United Nations University, 1984.

65. One of the other benefits frequently attributed to the economic policies of the Jayawardene government is a significant decline in unemployment rates. Seldom pointed out is that the new government 1) significantly increased public sector employment (on projects such as the massive Mahaweli dam scheme, among others); and 2) loosened restrictions on foreign travel and employment for indigenous Sri Lankans. Increased *private* investment was not the only—or even the principal—source of increased employment within Sri Lanka after 1977.

66. Whereas the poorest 20 percent of Sri Lankan households accounted for 7.5 percent of all household income in 1973, this figure had fallen to 3.8 percent in 1978/79. The wealthiest 10 percent of households, by contrast, showed a substantial gain over the same period, accounting for 28 percent of all income at the beginning of the decade and 39 percent at the end. AID, *A Comparative Analysis of Policies and Other Factors Which Affect the Role of the Private Sector in Economic Development,* AID Program Evaluation Discussion Paper, no. 20, Dec. 1983, 6–8. Evidence that income inequalities continued to grow through 1981/82, the last year for which data are available, can be found in: Gamini Abeysekera et al., *Sri Lanka: The Social Impact of Economic Policies During the Last Decade* (New York: UNICEF-Colombo, 1985), 22–23.

to capture these new benefits from a free market economy."[67]

Nutritional well-being has also been hurt. Inflation brought on by economic liberalization caused food prices to rise nearly 300 percent between 1977 and 1983,[68] while real wages and the value of government food stamps lagged far behind.[69] According to a 1985 UNICEF-sponsored report, between 1969/70 and 1981/82 the per capita calorie intake of the poorest ten percent of the population dropped by almost half, reaching less than 1200 calories a day.[70] On such a meager diet no adult can remain healthy.

Jamaica is another country touted for its return to the free market's fold. Following the 1980 election of conservative Prime Minister Edward Seaga, President Reagan advised the world to "watch Jamaica."[71] The Reagan administration boosted U.S. aid to Jamaica by more than 1,000 percent, from $14.4 million in 1980 to $164.6 million in 1985.[72] By 1986 Jamaica was the sixth largest per capita recipient of U.S. economic aid in the world.

President Seaga was being handsomely rewarded for embracing the free market prescriptions of the Reagan administration and the International Monetary Fund. He had removed price controls and cut consumer subsidies while keeping a lid on wages; made large cuts in government spend-

---

67. *Sri Lanka: The Impact of P.L. 480 Title I Food Assistance* AID Project Impact Evaluation Report, no. 39, Oct. 1982, app. D, D7.

68. These figures are based on Colombo only. The other available set of price increases shows a somewhat smaller decline, but is based on 1953 consumption patterns, which are less meaningful. For raw data and additional discussion, see Abeysekera et al., *Sri Lanka: The Social Impact,* chapter 4.

69. How much real wages actually declined depends, of course, on the price deflator one uses. See Ibid., 15–17 for more discussion of alternative deflators and their implications for real wage changes.

70. Ibid., chapters 4 and 5. For the next poorest ten percent of the population, caloric intake dropped from 2,065 calories/day to 1,558 over the same period.

71. The Resource Center, *Jamaica: Open for Business,* (Albuquerque, N.M.: The Resource Center, 1984).

72. AID, *Congressional Presentation, FY 1982,* main vol., 235; and *Congressional Presentation, FY 1987,* main vol., 668.

ing, especially social services; and created various incentives to encourage foreign capital to invest in the Jamaican economy.

Massive cuts in social spending did save the government money.[73] But layoffs and budget cuts in Jamaica's health and education systems—once among the best in the third world—have caused professionals to leave in droves, as we mentioned earlier. And the savings have not had much impact on Jamaica's debt crisis: payments on the national debt still soak up nearly one-third of all export earnings.[74]

Yes, some have benefited from the Seaga reforms. Jamaica's four largest banks (two foreign-owned) have seen their profits grow rapidly. But the economy as a whole is deteriorating: the economic growth rate in 1985—a year of recovery for many countries—was *negative* four percent.[75] The majority of Jamaicans have seen their living standards decline as prices soar, unemployment and crime increase, and fear and hopelessness come to dominate daily life.

Zaire "has been a model case in following IMF [and parallel AID] policy," notes the *The Christian Science Monitor,* "allowing its currency to fall and prices to rise, shrinking the size of government, lifting restrictions on imports, and paying its creditors on time."[76] Yet, after four years of following an IMF austerity program in order to make payments on its $5.4 billion foreign debt, Zaire's economy has deteriorated.

When the government loosened price controls, inflation

---

73. According to AID, by the end of 1985, some 12,000 public sector jobs will have been eliminated as a result of the Jamaican government's policy reforms. (See GAO, "U.S. Use of Conditions to Achieve Economic Reforms," report no. GAO/NSIAD-86-157, Aug. 1986), 58.

74. AID, *Congressional Presentation, FY 1987,* Latin America and the Caribbean, 270.

75. This refers to the decline in total Gross Domestic Product (GDP). The per capita decline in GDP was even greater—a negative 5.6 percent. See InterAmerican Development Bank, *Economic and Social Progress in Latin America 1986* (Washington, D.C.: InterAmerican Development Bank, 1986), table II-4, 17.

76. Barbara Bradley, " 'Model' Zaire Joins Countries Asking for Debt Restructuring," *The Christian Science Monitor,* Nov. 17, 1986, 10.

shot up to seventy-six percent, while workers' wages fell far behind. Zaire's ambassador to the United States admits: "Unemployment has risen and cutbacks in health care, education, child care, and other social programs are worrisome."[77]

Devaluation of the currency by ninety percent between 1983 and 1986 did help increase the volume of Zaire's exports, but the *value* of those exports fell by seventeen percent during the same period.[78] Zaire has been sending more money out of the country to creditors than it has received in new assistance. The formula just hasn't worked: in late 1986, the Zairean government was forced once again to seek rescheduling of its debt payments.

Because Zaire was so thoroughly compliant with western prescriptions for reform, and was hailed as a model reformer, its failure to escape economic stagnation holds significant lessons for other third-world countries.

Concluding Reflections:
Why AID's Formula Can't Work

Lest we be misunderstood as antimarket, we want to focus for a moment on its potential role in alleviating poverty. Since any society trying to do away with the market altogether has faced monumental headaches, the goal of well-functioning markets should be a key part of ending poverty and its worst symptom, hunger. But AID's formula has it backwards. It promotes the free market and entrepreneurs. But do they need promoting? Enterprising marketers spring up wherever there are customers. In much of the third world it's the customers who are missing. They, not the market, need to be promoted!

Customers are the engine of the market. They are what is missing where poverty is widespread. As the World Bank

---

77. Ibid.
78. Ibid.

itself acknowledges, hunger can only be alleviated "by redistributing purchasing power and resources toward those who are undernourished."[79] But U.S. foreign assistance must remain blind to this obvious truth, for to acknowledge it calls forth a further question: how do you generate more customers?

Government—made accountable by active citizenry—is the only agency through which wide dispersion of control over land, credit, and other essential resources can be achieved and maintained in order to generate customers for healthy markets. And here is the hitch for the free-market ideologues. Since they proscribe a significant role for government, and deem serious redistribution a communist plot, their *own* stated goal of healthy market economies is doomed. And so are the hungry.

When it comes to reform directly benefiting the poor majority, AID is suddenly silent. An AID-sponsored study of Guatemala—a country suffering from extreme land inequality—states forthrightly AID's excuse for not disturbing the powerful landowners.

> The United States risks ineffectiveness and counterproductive relations with a host government by getting ahead of the latter, in effect, finding itself in an out-front advocacy position, on sensitive domestic issues such as land reform. Questions concerning the character and pace of structural social and economic change in a country, as mirrored in an agrarian reform program, are best left to the host government.[80]

Similarly, even after pressure from citizens' groups forced AID to condition its aid to a number of countries on signs of progress toward respecting human rights (for example, the

---

79. World Bank, *Poverty and Hunger: Issues and Options for Food Security in Developing Countries* (Washington, D.C.: World Bank, 1986), 49.

80. AID, *Land and Labor in Guatemala: An Assessment* (Washington, D.C.: Agency for International Development, 1982), 51.

right to organize free labor unions in Haiti), we find little evidence that such conditions are being enforced.

AID apparently sees no contradiction between its squeamishness on pushing land reform or the rights of workers and its strong advocacy position when it comes to privatization or devaluation. Pushing for redistribution of wealth and power downward is off limits, but pushing for redistribution upward is seen as an all-purpose cure for economic ills.

THE MISSING INGREDIENTS

While economic policy reform is often badly needed, AID-promoted privatization and export expansion cannot solve the basic economic problems of the third world. Leaving unaddressed the extreme inequalities in access to resources, they do not help create the economic *preconditions* for sustained development.

To review the themes of this chapter: we believe that there are at least two such preconditions. Contrary to AID's formula thinking, the issue is not simply one of intervening or not intervening in the marketplace. All governments are involved in the economy. The key question is *how* a government intervenes—in whose interest does it operate?

Not to pay adequate prices for agricultural goods, to discriminate against family farmers in favor of urban dwellers, and to tolerate inefficient and sometimes corrupt government bureaucracies—all this *must* change. But aren't these problems really symptoms of an underlying one—the lack of a democratically accountable structure of government? If so, then most of AID's reforms could contribute to genuine development only as part of change involving greater accountability to majority interests. This is the first precondition.

The second, inseparable precondition for economic reforms to alleviate poverty is a broadening of access to resources and purchasing power. Countries of vastly different political persuasions (Japan, South Korea, North Korea, Zimbabwe,

China, and Taiwan) have shown that redistribution of access to farmland, for example, can significantly boost economic development. But AID, as we have seen, demands sweeping reforms to strengthen the business sector, while refusing to press for changes such as land reform which would begin this broadening process.

The sad truth is that no simple formula will stimulate broad-based development. As long as AID's prescription leaves out the prior political questions of government accountability and the distribution of purchasing power, its program of privatization, export expansion, and luring private investment cannot produce the promised economic revitalization. Unwilling to address the preconditions to genuine development we have discussed here—involving the democratization of economic life—AID's reform package can only strengthen the very forces that have so impoverished the third world.

In the failure of AID's economic formula most Americans lose, too, and not just in our misappropriated tax dollars. As AID's approach reinforces the distortion of third-world economies to serve wealthy minorities, Americans lose millions of potential customers for goods we export. The majority there will remain too poor to stimulate demand. Since AID's economic program fails to give priority to workers' rights, it also cannot help ease the threat to American jobs and wages posed by third-world workers whose survival requires that they work for a tiny fraction of U.S. wages. Thus, any policy that fails to get at the root of poverty abroad fails us as well.

Six

Foreign Aid and American Security: The Real Threat

The less developed nations of the world will be the principal U.S.-Soviet battleground for many years to come.

—CIA DIRECTOR WILLIAM CASEY, 1983.[1]

AND ON THAT BATTLEGROUND, the U.S. government sees its foreign aid as a potent weapon. So military aid comes to overwhelm other types of assistance. Our tax dollars flow to governments least likely to use them to benefit their poor. U.S. food aid serves narrowly defined security interests. And foreign-aid leverage gets used to bend recipient nations to U.S. free-market ideology.

Sure, compromises are involved, we are told. In the real world they are unavoidable. We are, after all, in a life-and-death struggle against a Soviet campaign to subvert and to subjugate third-world governments. Compromises—supporting brutal dictators or even stooping to terrorism ourselves—are acceptable because they serve our much larger crusade for freedom against an "evil empire."

1. *The Soviet Union in the Third World, 1980–85: An Imperial Burden or Political Asset?* Congressional Research Service, Library of Congress, prepared for the Committee on Foreign Affairs, U.S. House of Representatives, Sept. 23, 1985, 459.

Does this rationale for the current direction of U.S. aid hold up? In answering this question, assessing the magnitude of the Soviet threat is the all important first step.

THE SCOPE OF SOVIET INFLUENCE

Twenty leading specialists on the Soviet Union convened at the U.S. Army War College in 1979. The volume of their presentations to the conference begins with this summary of their views: "The influence of the U.S.S.R. in the third world remains limited. . . . U.S. policymakers should not overestimate the Soviet's appeal."[2] Since then, a number of studies suggest that Soviet influence has, if anything, declined even further. A 1986 study notes that Soviet influence is substantial now only in eleven percent of the world's nations, down from a peak in the 1950s of fifteen percent.[3]

Notwithstanding this unimpressive record, our government tells us that the Soviet Union menaces us and the rest of the world—especially the weaker nations of the third world. Its communist doctrine insists that revolution abroad must be instigated and led by Marxist-Leninist parties. Once such parties win power, they will move on an inexorable track toward Soviet-style communism and become steadfast Soviet allies.

Notably few experts accept this scenario. To Brookings Institution Sovietologist Jerry Hough, such "Stalinist orthodoxy" is still believed by only a handful of people who can be found not in Moscow but in Washington! Hough writes: "Paradoxically, [this] old Stalinist orthodoxy that has been

2. Robert H. Donaldson, ed., *The Soviet Union in the Third World: Success and Failures* (Boulder, Col.: Westview Press, 1981), frontispiece. The conference was held under the auspices of the Strategic Studies Institute.

3. *Soviet Geopolitical Momentum: Myth or Menace? Trends of Soviet Influence Around the World From 1945 to 1986.* The Defense Monitor, vol. 15, no. 5, 1986, 1. See also Richard J. Barnet, "Why Trust the Soviets?" *World Policy Journal,* Spring 1984. He writes: "Soviet influence in the third world is near an all-time low. The Soviet economic model is neither widely admired nor widely imitated." (476)

almost universally abandoned in the Soviet Union still retains a strong hold in the United States."[4] Hough continues:

> Few [Soviet] scholars assume that a third world leader's profession of allegiance to Marxism-Leninism or "scientific socialism" should necessarily be taken at face value. . . . No one believes that radical revolutions inevitably proceed toward Soviet socialism. Indeed, most Soviet scholars are so eager for major reform of the Soviet economic system that they do not even advise third world countries to adopt it.[5]

Washington would have us believe, nonetheless, that the Soviet Union is hungrily scanning the globe looking for insurgencies it can transform into Marxist-Leninist vanguards tied to Moscow. If correct, why has Moscow ignored the New People's Army in the Philippines? The NPA surely would be a likely target for Soviet takeover, given the close relationship between the Philippines and the United States. Yet, two decades after its founding, the NPA remains an indigenous force, unsupported by outside aid.[6] (Ironically, as the communist NPA was leading the armed opposition to Ferdinand Marcos, the Soviet Union in 1985 honored him with an award as a "hero of the Second World War"!)

If the Soviet Union is so eager for new clients, why did Chile under Salvador Allende (1970–1973) receive little more than token Soviet support?[7] And how does Washington's view of ever-extending Soviet power jibe with Zim-

---

4. Jerry F. Hough, *The Struggle for the Third World: Soviet Debates and American Options* (Washington, D.C.: The Brookings Institution, 1986), 281.

5. Ibid., 281.

6. *The Situation in the Philippines,* U.S. Senate Foreign Relations Committee, Sept. 1984. See also: Walden Bello, "The Rebirth of the Philippine Revolution: A Review Essay," *Third World Quarterly,* Jan. 1986. The main source of supply has been arms captured in the field from the Philippine military.

7. Paul E. Sigmund, "The USSR, Cuba, and the Revolution in Chile," in Donaldson, ed., *The Soviet Union in the Third World.* 33ff.

babwe's revolutionary history? Joshua Nkomo's ZAPU party was unable to gain primary leadership of the liberation movement, despite massive Soviet backing. Its rival ZANU played a bigger role in the war and was elected to govern the new Zimbabwe after liberation—all with little Soviet help.[8]

U.S. foreign aid policy is justified to block Soviet expansionism which seeks the violent overthrow of legitimate governments by armed Marxist-Leninist revolutionaries. But in Chile, Nicaragua, and other Latin American countries, communist parties supported by the Soviet Union have been opposed to armed struggle.[9]

Moreover, the view promoted by Washington—that once a nation comes under Soviet influence it remains so forever—could not pass an undergraduate history test. Consider, for example, Soviet loss of influence in such significant third-world nations as China (1960), Indonesia (1962), Egypt (1972), India (1977), and Iraq (1978). Of the nine African nations significantly influenced by the U.S.S.R. in the postwar era, only Ethiopia, Angola, and Mozambique remain in that category,[10] and in Mozambique Soviet influence is waning. "Even in the alleged heyday of 'Soviet geopolitical momentum' during the 1970s Soviet losses nearly equaled gains," reports the Center for Defense Information.[11] Clearly, billions of rubles in aid to these countries did not buy loyalty. The same point can be made about U.S. aid dollars.

In assessing the effectiveness of an aggressive U.S. policy against Soviet expansion, it's also worth remembering that in most instances Soviet losses have been unrelated to specific American actions. The split between the Soviet Union and

---

8. Kevin Danaher, *In Whose Interest?: A Guide to U.S.-South Africa Relations* (Washington, D.C.: Institute for Policy Studies, 1984), 90 ff. Section on "The Limits of Soviet Power."

9. *The Soviet Union in the Third World: 1980–1985,* Congressional Research Service, 319. On Chile, see *The Soviet Union in the Third World: Successes and Failures,* 34ff.

10. *Soviet Geopolitical Momentum,* 11.

11. Ibid., 5.

China in the early 1960s is the most dramatic case in point.[12] In Africa there are at least a half dozen examples of such Soviet losses, including Egypt, Somalia, and Ghana. In several critical instances—Vietnam, Cuba, and Angola—aggressive U.S. policies have actually ended up solidifying Soviet influence. The Nicaraguan government, responding to U.S. aggression and pressure on western allies not to sell arms to Nicaragua, has turned to the Soviets for assistance.

A critical distinction must be made here. That the Soviet Union will seize an opportunity to gain prestige and influence in the third world goes without saying. But this is quite different from arguing, as Washington does, that all revolutionary movements and governments in the world are the products of Soviet subversion.

The Reagan doctrine further assumes that Soviet involvement in any country is an asset to it and therefore a detriment to us. But many countries under Soviet influence are tiny and poverty-stricken. Some have greatly sapped the Soviet treasury. Castro has been "sufficiently expensive for Moscow to avoid taking on a similar burden elsewhere," noted specialist in Soviet affairs, Joseph Nogee, while a visiting professor at the U.S. Army War College.[13] In fact, the economic burden imposed by their third-world allies has moved the U.S.S.R. to reduce its aid. Soviet arms sales, for example, are on much less lenient terms than in the past. Economic necessity has also made the Soviet Union much less ideologically picky about where it invests its resources. Countries that can pay in hard currency—Algeria or Morocco, for example—are favored over poorer socialist-oriented states.[14] Morocco's King Has-

---

12. The Sino-Soviet split was touched off by the U.S.S.R. backing down on an earlier agreement to share nuclear weapons technology with China. See Herbert Franz Schurmann, *The Logic of World Power: An Inquiry Into the Origins, Currents and Contradictions of World Politics* (New York: Pantheon, 1974).

13. *The Soviet Union in the Third World: Success and Failures,* 439.

14. Carol R. Saivetz and Sylvia Woodby, *Soviet-Third World Relations* (Boulder, Col.: Westview Press, 1985), 135–136. Saivetz is a fellow at Harvard University's Russian Research Center. Woodby is chairman of the International Relations Program at Goucher College.

san "is far from radical, yet the Soviet Union has made its largest third world investment in this Middle East monarchy," note two authorities on Soviet involvement in the third world.[15]

Beyond Zero-Sum: Third World Nations' Drive for Sovereignty

Regardless, don't Soviet actions in the third world—especially in Africa and close to U.S. shores in Latin America—confirm an alarming pattern of subversion of pro-Western governments? Doesn't this subversion justify U.S. aid, no matter how unsavory the regime in power?

First, such a view assumes that just because a pro-Western government falls, the new government will become subservient to the Soviet Union if it assisted that government's rise to power. In this zero-sum view of world politics, third-world people can choose only between two outside powers. It assumes that after shedding decades or even centuries of colonial rule, third-world nations will allow themselves again to fall under the control of another foreign power.

But, as a 1985 Congressional Research Service study points out: "It must be recognized that neither the U.S. nor Soviet forms of social organization and ideology may be acceptable to the nations of the Third World who have their own interests to satisfy."[16] Even the CIA agrees:

> Reduced Western influence in Third World countries has not necessarily led to corresponding rise in Soviet influence. New governments often have translated anticoloni-

---

15. Ibid., 193. The reason for the U.S.S.R's keen interest is Morocco's large deposits of phosphates, needed for fertilizing the troubled farm sector of the Soviet economy.

16. *The Soviet Union in the Third World, 1980–85,* 460.

alist positions into strong nationalist policies jealous of any foreign influence.[17]

Washington often uses Angola, Libya, and Nicaragua as evidence of Soviet expansionism and control over its client-states. What does the record show? While the Soviets have delivered $3.5 billion in weapons to Angola, they have been denied permanent military bases there. The United States remains Angola's major trading partner. As for Libya, the Center for Defense Information notes that the U.S.S.R. finds "Qaddafi impossible to manage or control."[18] Qaddafi's "green book," which lays out his political and economic philosophy, is as tough on communism as on capitalism. But in the 1980s, Nicaragua has become Washington's proof that the Soviets are nipping at our heels. "If we permit the Soviets, using the Sandinistas, to establish a beachhead on the American mainland," President Reagan warned in 1985, "We could turn around one day and find a string of pro-Soviet dictatorships in Central America and a threat to our southern borders."[19]

In fact, the Soviet Union did not support the Sandinistas in their effort to overthrow Somoza. The Soviets supported a Nicaraguan communist party that had opposed the Sandinistas, signed a pact with Somoza, and *still* are part of the opposition within Nicaragua today. Even after all-out efforts by Washington to isolate the country from the West, less than a third of Nicaragua's trade in 1985 was with the Eastern Bloc.[20] While the President of Nicaragua has gone to the

---

17. Cited in Orah Cooper and Carol Fogarty, "Soviet and Economic and Military Aid to Less Developed Countries, 1958–1978," Joint Economic Committee, *Soviet Economy in a Time of Change.* pt. 2, 1979, 657.

18. *Soviet Geopolitical Momentum,* 20.

19. Apr. 18, 1985, quoted in "Nicaragua in Quotes," *The Progressive Review,* #256, May–June 1986, 15.

20. Based on figures from the Nicaraguan Ministry of Foreign Trade, interview with the Central American Historical Institute, Intercultural Center, Georgetown University.

Soviet Union in search of aid, no high Soviet official has ever visited Nicaragua, and the Soviet Union appears determined to avoid any statement that would require it to protect Nicaragua against U.S. attack. Peru receives twice as much Soviet as U.S. aid[21] and there are twice as many Soviet military advisors in Peru as in Nicaragua.[22] Yet who would argue that the Soviets are determining Peru's policies?

Washington would have us believe that U.S. threats are all that's now preventing the Soviets from building a military base in Nicaragua. If that's our government's real fear, surely it has the intelligence capabilities to detect such a Soviet move and block it. But such a notion fails to answer a prior question: why would *Nicaragua* permit it? Sergio Ramirez Mercado, Nicaragua's vice-president, asks:

> What benefit would there be for us in allowing the Soviets to come in and establish a foreign military base here? . . . It is impossible [for the U.S.] to imagine a country without military bases of *either* superpower on its soil or a small country that will not bow to the strategic interests of a great one.[23]

Ramirez is adamant that "Nicaragua will not be a strategic reserve for anyone" and reminds Americans that his government has offered the United States written proposals and draft treaties to that effect.[24]

21. U.S. Agency for International Development, *Congressional Presentation for Security Assistance Programs, Fiscal Year 1987,* vol. 1, 10.

22. *Soviet Geopolitical Momentum,* 30, 31.

23. Sergio Ramirez Mercado, "On Nicaragua's Resolve," *World Policy Journal,* Spring 1984, 672.

24. Ibid.

U.S. Aid: Buying Us Security?

If Soviet expansionism appears grossly overdrawn by our government to justify U.S. foreign aid, what of Washington's more positive declaration, that its foreign aid strategy will buy us allies, enchancing our security?

As noted in our opening chapter, many of the U.S. government's long-standing allies, into which it has poured billions of foreign aid dollars, have been overthrown, just since the early 1970s: these include the Shah of Iran, Somoza of Nicaragua, Marcos of the Philippines, and Haile Selassie in Ethiopia.[25] Today, major aid recipients such as Pakistan, Zaire, Honduras, and El Salvador have little or no more popular support than did those deposed regimes.

And, just as Soviet aid does not make third-world nations into mere instruments of Soviet policy, so U.S. aid does not enable Washington easily to set its clients' foreign policies. In Sudan, for example, significant U.S. aid has not prevented that country in recent years from working to improve links with Ethiopia and Libya, archenemies of the United States. Despite massive U.S. aid to Central American countries (excluding Nicaragua, of course), as of late 1986 none would openly permit the United States to train contra forces on their soil to overthrow the government of Nicaragua.

Security specialist Richard Barnet exposes the futility of superpower attempts at control of developments in the third world:

> As evidenced by the U.S. experience in El Salvador and Lebanon and by the Soviet experience in Afghanistan, [military intervention] no longer serves political objectives in the way it once did. Both superpowers are losing the control over small nations they once had. The inde-

---

25. Others include Lon Nol of Cambodia (now Kampuchea), Thieu of South Vietnam, Tolbert of Liberia, Duvalier of Haiti, and Numieri of Sudan.

pendent forces that operate in critical areas—tribes, religious sects, political factions—defy orchestration from outside.[26]

A further rationale for U.S. foreign aid is that only through keeping third-world nations in our camp will doors remain open for investments by U.S. corporations. Once more, historical experience fails to bear this out.

Let's take Nicaragua again, since it is such a sticking point for U.S. policymakers. Research faculty of the Harvard Business School studying multinational companies operating in Nicaragua—including ESSO, Chevron, Monsanto, and United Brands—concluded that, since the fall of Somoza, many of these firms have not only survived but grown, in spite of a U.S.-enforced trade embargo.[27] The one foreign company that the Nicaraguan government has expropriated was compensated, and only one foreign company had withdrawn from Nicaragua as of 1984.[28]

The absurdity of the view that noncapitalist economies will automatically exclude U.S. firms was brought home in 1986. News reports described Cuban troops guarding Chevron installations in Marxist Angola—protecting them from attack by *U.S.*-supported guerrillas! Earlier that year, Business International, a U.S. consulting firm, described the Angolan Government as "a reliable business partner and one who values the role of foreign business and understands companies' needs to make a profit."[29]

Moreover, as we pointed out in chapter 1, the United States trades with many communist countries and U.S. corporations maintain profitable investments from China to Ethiopia.

---

26. Barnet, "Why Trust the Soviets?" 478.

27. James E. Austin and John C. Ickis, "Managing After the Revolutionaries Have Won," *Harvard Business Review,* May–June 1986, 103–109.

28. Ramirez, "On Nicaragua's Resolve," 673.

29. James Brooke, "Policy Aside, America Does Business as Usual with Angola," *The New York Times,* Nov. 30, 1986, E3.

Imperial Policy Backfires

Both the United States and the Soviet Union have seen heavy-
handed attempts to use foreign aid to buy influence in the
third world backfire. Rather than increasing these superpowers' stature and influence, such policies have actually undermined their credibility and cost them economically as well.

Consider the Soviet Union in Afghanistan. Dependent on
the Soviet Union since 1954, Afghanistan has received almost
all its military aid and two-thirds of its economic aid from the
U.S.S.R. These aid ties made Soviet leaders believe that by
sending in over 100,000 troops, they could successfully prop
up a military regime with little popular support. For this, the
Soviet Union has paid a heavy price, not only in the loss of
Soviet lives and billions of rubles, but in damaged prestige
among many nonaligned nations. And it has allowed the
United States and China to project themselves as disinterested
defenders of freedom.

While the United States has not sent U.S. troops into combat in Central America, its massive military buildup in the
region, including the shoring up of unpopular governments,
and the attempt to overthrow an elected government in
Nicaragua, has similarly caused a loss of U.S. stature. When
the United States imposed trade sanctions against Nicaragua,
for example, not a single European ally followed suit, and
many expressed strong disapproval.[30]

When the United States makes fear of the Soviet Union the
operative—indeed, virtually the only—guide in policy deci-
sions, it alienates third-world people and appears unconcerned
about their legitimate demands. The United States backed the
white minorities in the former Portuguese colonies in Africa,
for example, accepting their simplistic labeling of black nation-

---

30. Daniel Siegel and Tom Spaulding, *Outcast Among Allies* (Washington, D.C.:
Institute for Policy Studies, 1985), 9ff.

alist opposition movements as communist and extreme. (Yet, after coming to power, they have proved quite reasonable.) By linking Washington to racist South Africa, even token U.S. assistance now going to South Africa-backed guerrillas attempting to overthrow the Angolan government puts the United States in a bad light. The Organization of African Unity and the 100-member Non-Aligned Movement have strongly denounced the policy.

U.S. policies in other regions have similarly heightened anti-American sentiment. Charles Lister, an American who went to Pakistan in late 1984 as a member of the Lawyers Committee for International Human Rights, wrote of the hatred that many Pakistanis feel toward their government's chief benefactor, the United States.

> Many Pakistanis believe that their problems are partly our creation. One told me that "U.S. aid is the crutch that supports Zia." Our government's encouragement is blamed for Islamization and even [ex-President] Bhutto's execution.
>
> Some bitterly accused us of being more eager to embarrass the Soviets in Afghanistan than to condemn Zia's abuses. "When Zia falls," one warned, "more American flags will be burned here than in Iran."[31]

The Unspoken Threat

Our own observations, coupled with all we have learned from scholars studying Soviet policy, suggest that the stated rationale for U.S. foreign aid does not pass the test of history or logic. Typically, when a reaction is grossly disproportionate to a real threat, or when a rhetorical explanation doesn't square

---

31. Charles Lister, "America Can Help Pakistan Avoid Violence–Or Worse," *The Lost Angeles Times,* Dec. 26, 1984, pt. 2, 5.

with actual events, one looks for alternative explanations. Thus, U.S. foreign aid policies, and the rhetoric defending them, leave us asking: What does Washington really fear? Why does its worldview distort the historical record summarized here in order to hold to a caricature of the Soviet Union's behavior in the third world?

Thus far we have built our argument on historical evidence, but to answer this question—what *motivates* U.S. policy?—facts aren't enough. One can only hypothesize, and then continually weigh which explanation best fits unfolding events.

One theory starts with the "Vietnam syndrome," suggesting that the U.S. defeat in Southeast Asia so weakened the nation's confidence in military solutions to foreign policy confrontations that the military establishment was thrown on the defensive. Spotting a Soviet threat behind every insurgency (or less-than-friendly foreign government) has been the only way the military could convince the American people to accept its expanded authority and spending, *especially* during an era of declining real income for most American workers.

We do not reject this theory. We think it can help to explain the Reagan administration's policies. But the policies we describe in this book are not limited to the eighties; many predate the Vietnam War. For us, the only way to fully comprehend U.S. policies toward the third world is to posit what we call "the threat of a good example." Insurgencies in the third world do not challenge U.S. military security or even, ultimately, investments by U.S. corporations, as we have seen. What they represent is the possibility that emerging nations may demonstrate by example that the United States may not be the last word in democracy, freedom, and opportunity. That threat is much greater if weighed from the perspective of those who see it in their interest to preserve unchanged the present U.S. economic and political order.

This might sound farfetched. But think of the implications. What if a third-world society demonstrated that the choice is not just between U.S.-style capitalism and Soviet-style statism? What if an emerging third-world order were to offer *greater* opportunities for citizens to be involved in the shaping of economic policy than either superpower model—more worker-owned businesses, independent farming cooperatives, as well as citizen participation in village to national economic planning? Or expanded human rights protection to include the right of every rural person to farmland sufficient to live in dignity? Or began building a political system in which wealth is strictly precluded as a factor in gaining office?

We are not talking about utopias. We don't believe in them. We are simply talking about societies trying to do things somewhat differently than we do here, based on different underlying assumptions. To U.S. policymakers, only the market distribution of goods and exclusively private control over productive property are consistent with freedom and democracy. To do things differently is to undermine both. But what if an emerging society were to question such a dogmatic approach to the market and private control, putting people's need for land, jobs, and food first? And what if such policies were pursued with broad popular support, not repressive measures, so that people felt their freedom expanded?

Such a development almost certainly would give hope to oppressed peoples throughout the world who today have so few positive examples to inspire them. Moreover, U.S. citizens, observing these developments abroad, might be encouraged to challenge the control of concentrated wealth here at home and the assumption that those monolithic corporations so determining our well-being are best left beyond democratic control. It should be noted that the concentration of wealth in the United States is no less than in many third-world countries. Here, the richest one percent own more wealth than the bottom ninety percent.[32]

---

32. The top one percent of Americans have 34.2 percent of net worth; the bottom 90 percent, 32.1 percent of net worth. Unpublished survey by the University of Michigan Survey Research Center for the Board of Governors of the Federal Reserve

In this sense, the "domino effect" may be a legitimate fear, for some. Not that dominoes fall into the Soviet camp, but that, if there were just one third-world society to offer both greater freedom grounded in economic security, along with civil liberties, it would inspire others to work to challenge the control of concentrated wealth.

Our government constantly rivets public attention on the Soviet Union as the only real threat to our well-being. This approach serves beautifully to insure that such embarrassing questions are not raised. And, at the same time, it insures—through militarized foreign policies described in this book—that no third-world society that might provoke such questions is allowed to emerge.

Common Interests

Above we proposed that a U.S. policy supporting repressive governments and subverting those with Soviet ties ends up backfiring, in some cases even strengthening the position of the Soviet Union. But in a broader sense, we believe these policies ultimately defeat the interests of the majority of Americans as well. As long as the United States contributes to maintaining political structures in the third world that trap people in poverty, it undercuts the well-being of U.S. citizens. How? To answer, we must first ask: On what does the well-being of most Americans rest?

First, peace and security. But can there be peace as long as people are deprived of survival necessities? Throughout the world, the 20th century has seen the concept of human rights deepen to embrace the notion of economic justice. In part through religious awakening, in part through growing aware-

System. For international comparisons, see, for example: *World Development Report 1986* (New York: Oxford University Press, 1986), table 24.

ness that sufficient resources do exist for all, people who have been robbed of life-sustaining resources are demanding *economic* rights: land to feed their families, jobs, food. (An irony is that in part it is *American* rhetoric of freedom and democracy that has helped to inspire this spreading belief in a better future.)

Such people, long oppressed but awakening to their rights, will not be silenced. Thus, unless their rights are acknowledged, violence will continue to mount. Our point is simple: it takes violence to keep people hungry. Americans want to live in a less volatile world, but are denied this greater security, as long as Washington's low intensity warfare blocks real change in the third world.

Second, bargaining power as workers. In an economy dominated by globe-spanning corporations, neither the jobs nor wages of American workers are secure, as long as hundreds of millions of workers in the third world are denied the right to organize. Until workers can organize and establish links of mutual support across national borders, corporations are free to go wherever they can find the most inexpensive and pliant workforce. And, they can always threaten to, and often do, go elsewhere if workers demand a living wage and healthy working conditions.

Third, markets for their production. As long as majorities abroad are kept in poverty, U.S. workers are denied millions of customers for our exports. And, as long as third-world countries are ruled by elite-controlled governments eager to push food exports while their own people go without, U.S. farmers will be increasingly squeezed out of international markets. Today, for example, markets for U.S. farmers' commodities abroad are being undercut in part by rapidly increasing exports from Latin American countries.[33]

In these and many other ways the interests of the vast major-

---

33. "The Impact of the Latin American Debt Crisis on the U.S. Economy," a staff study prepared for the use of the Joint Economic Committee, Congress of the United States, May 10, 1986.

ity in the United States are not served by a keep-the-lid-on-change foreign aid policy. Our interests can be met only as profound changes occur that begin to democratize political *and* economic life within third world societies.

This is not to say that some would not lose in such a redirection of our foreign aid policy. The primary losers here would be among the 30,000 U.S. companies now engaged in military production, the demand for which is fueled by current U.S. policies. A less militarized foreign policy would surely mean fewer jobs in the arms industry; wouldn't this undercut the well-being of American workers?

Money transferred from the military budget to the civilian economy would minimally generate the same number of jobs; and compared to investments in weapons development, civilian spending creates *more* jobs.[34] Moreover, many economists believe that the militarization of our economy is contributing directly to America's economic decline, because high military expenditures are linked to low productivity growth. (And productivity—output per worker—is essential to increased real income.) The United States ranks first in military spending but last in productivity growth among nine industrial capitalist countries,[35] in part because nearly seventy percent of all federal research money now goes to the military.[36]

FOR THE LONG HAUL

In even broaching such far-reaching issues, we are, in effect, saying that those who want to make a difference in changing U.S. foreign policy must be "in it for the long haul." The policies described in our book did not originate in the 1980s.

34. Ann Markusen, "The Militarized Economy," *World Policy Journal,* Summer 1986. See also: L. J. Griffin, M. Wallace and J. Devine, "Political Economy of Military Spending," *Cambridge Journal of Economics,* 1982, no. 6, 1–14.

35. Ruth Leger Sivard, *World Military and Social Expenditures 1986* (Washington, D.C.: World Priorities, 1986), 20.

36. "Militarism in America," *The Defense Monitor,* vol. 15, no. 3, 3.

Today's foreign aid program is merely an extreme version of what went before.

What Americans must undertake is nothing less than a re-thinking of the very definition of our national interest. We must become ever more articulate in explaining that a foreign policy based on the moral and logical inconsistencies we document in this book cannot mean greater security to us.

And such a change is possible only, we believe, through broad educational initiatives. Offering alternative sources of information and analysis to one's representatives in Washington is the first step. Working to put people in office whose positions reflect a deeper understanding of security than the policies now pursued is equally important, but neither is enough. Profound change can only emerge as we reach out even more broadly to awaken people to new ways of thinking—in our communities, churches, schools, workplaces, and through the media. Ultimately, pressure will mount in Washington only as more and more Americans know what is being perpetrated in their names, and against their own interests.

We must work to encourage Americans to ask: What would be the basis of a constructive foreign aid policy? We believe that three premises follow from the analysis presented in this book:

- *Our own security is enhanced by overcoming our government's fear of change abroad.*   No longer allowing our government to prop up dictators blocking change (who use the cry of communist subversion to ensure U.S. backing), we can find hope and inspiration ourselves in the efforts of third world people to change their societies. To overcome fear of change, we can learn from history. At the time of China's revolution, policymakers could think of nothing more foreboding to our interests than "losing" China. Yet a few decades later, China is a valued U.S. trading partner and recognition of its independence from control by either superpower is a stabilizing force in the world.

- *In the late 20th century, a nation's influence arises more from economic than military strength.* "Geoeconomics is replacing geopolitics," note World Policy Institute analysts Sherle R. Schwenninger and Jerry W. Sanders. "Economic strength and political dialogue, not military might, increasingly determine a nation's power and influence—its ability to shape events, and to build a world order compatible with its values."[37] China and Japan seem to grasp this reality, but not the United States. While the United States was becoming a debtor nation, Japan's net foreign assets leapt twelvefold to $125 billion, just since 1980. And Japan is predicted to displace the United States in 1988 as the world's leading trading power.[38]

Noting a sixty-five percent increase in real defense expenditures between 1981 and 1987, Schwenninger and Sanders write:

> By devoting a larger portion of U.S. resources and talent to military competition at the expense of the economy, the Reagan administration and for that matter the Carter administration before it, have eroded America's national economic strength, and thus its foreign policy position.[39]

Their well-put insight brings us to our final point concerning the basis of a constructive international role for the United States.

- *Genuine development cannot be imported or imposed; it can only be achieved by a people for themselves.* This final premise has profound implications. It suggests that, at best, foreign aid can support initiatives for change that are already underway by people able to define their own means and goals.

---

37. Sherle R. Schwenninger and Jerry W. Sanders, "The Democrats and a New Grand Strategy," *World Policy Journal.* Summer 1986, 373–374.

38. Lester R. Brown, "Redefining National Security: The Superpowers," Worldwatch Features, 1776 Massachusetts Ave. N.W., Washington, D.C. 20036, 1986.

39. Schwenninger and Sanders, "The Democrats," 375.

It also suggests that among our greatest contributions to the cause of freedom and development overseas is not what we do over there, but what we do right here at home. In contributing what is best about America—including lessons from our long history of political democracy—we are bound to fail if we try to push our ideas down the throats of others. Freedom and democracy, by their very nature, can arise only as people themselves infuse these values into their own societies.

With the world's oldest political democracy, America should be a beacon of hope. But, emerging leadership in the third world can hardly be expected to find inspiration in our example, if we—with average incomes 100 times or more what they have—tolerate widespread and growing poverty, hunger, and homelessness. Thus, only as we address the roots of needless suffering of millions of poor Americans can we offer our most important contribution to the third world.

Upon these three premises a constructive foreign aid policy could be built. Its goal would be a redirection of U.S. aid away from governments actively blocking changes necessary to alleviate the poverty and hunger of their people. It would be grounded in the assumption that foreign aid cannot effectively control governments seeking to break free from domination by both superpowers. And it would understand that just because another economic or political structure is not like ours, it does not have to aid or become our enemy. Most important, it would acknowledge that a foreign aid policy built upon both logical and moral contradictions cannot serve the American people.

Afterword

What Can We Do?
A Question of
Responsibility

RESPONSIBILITY is often a synonym for blame. It is used to point fingers and lay on the guilt. Responsibility also carries with it the notion of *a capacity to respond,* and it is this positive meaning of the word that we want to stress. Millions of Americans, we believe, want to respond. Especially after the 1986 scandals linking clandestine arms sales to Iran to illegal funds for the contras in Nicaragua, more than ever, Americans see the need to bring foreign policy under democratic control. But how do we respond effectively?

First, we must be regularly informed. Getting key information is essential. In addition to our own Institute's materials we suggest below other periodicals providing the background one needs to take informed action.

Let America Know

In our conclusion we pointed out the most obvious and important step for Americans—to let their representatives hear their views. But this is not possible unless Americans know what is being done in their names and with their tax dollars. With the knowledge gained through such educational resources and organizations as those listed below, one can work to awaken Americans to the shame of current U.S. foreign aid.

Many of the public education projects of the Institute for Food and Development Policy (also called Food First) have reinforced our view that Americans *will* act, once they see the impact of U.S. foreign policy, unfiltered by Washington. One particular experience, however, stands out. In 1985, we co-sponsored a project which produced a documentary film for television—*Faces of War*—on U.S. policies in Central America. Initially, it was banned by virtually all major stations, but through tremendous public pressure, doors opened, and it has now been aired on fifty stations. The film project has become a separate organization called Neighbor to Neighbor.

Organizers for Neighbor to Neighbor are using the film successfully in dozens of communities throughout the nation. It has been part of effective campaigns shaping congressional votes on aid to Central American governments. If you would like to become part of this campaign, write to Neighbor to Neighbor, whose address is listed below.

Our initial difficulties in airing *Faces of War* remind us that essential to changing U.S. foreign policy is insuring that critical voices—including those most hurt by it—are allowed to be heard within the United States.

During the Reagan presidency, the (McCarthy-era) McCarran-Walter Immigration Act, has been dusted off and used to keep critics and others out, almost 700 in 1984 alone. Noted writer Margaret Randall is now threatened with deportation for her critical views on U.S. foreign policy. Nobel laureates Carlos Fuentes and Gabriel García Márquez have been barred from our country, along with the widow of Salvador Allende and high-level Nicaraguan officials. In 1986, U.S. immigration authorities seized, held without charges, and then deported Colombian journalist Patricia Lara who has written critically about U.S. policies in Central America. (Lara had been invited to our country by Columbia University to receive an award for excellence in journalism!) Abolishing the McCarran-Walter Act is vital because it will allow Americans to understand the impact of U.S. policies.

Alternatives to the Peace Corps

But what about direct work abroad? Can't we do more to help? Our answer is yes, but we must preface our response by reminding ourselves that development—as chapter 3 stresses—does not start with outside aid, no matter how well-intended. In every country in the world people are struggling to build organizations in their communities in order to improve their lives. Our Institute publishes a short guide to groups that offer work opportunities with such initiatives. We call it *Alternatives to the Peace Corps,* which you can order from our address below.

But even if you cannot work abroad, one of the most important steps that any American can take is a step across our borders—a lengthy visit to the third world. Seeing U.S. policies from the vantage point of others offers insights that can shape one's perspective for a lifetime. Several U.S. organizations lead study tours to third-world countries, introducing visitors to local economic and political realities. We've included several such tour groups below.

Voluntary Contributions

In addition, financial contributions can support indigenous efforts, but they must be channeled through groups which are in touch with grass-roots movements and have the sensitivity to help without overwhelming local organizers with outside influence. Our short list of such groups which follows is a place to start. It is not an exhaustive listing, only a suggestion of the types of organizations you might want to learn more about.

Since the 1970s, the number of groups and individuals working to change U.S. foreign policy has grown markedly, especially within the religious community. Our hope is that this book will build on these courageous initiatives, so that more Americans will see the need to mold a new foreign policy, one worthy of our nation's highest ideals.

The Long Haul: Working with Youth

We hope our book makes clear that the challenge is not only to change current U.S. foreign policy, but also to rethink our understanding of development, both here and abroad. Vital in this process is reaching out to young people, as their ideas about the possibilities for change are first being formed. Thus, our Institute has produced two curricula, for both grade school and high school, that help children understand the roots of hunger and to think critically about development. The high school curriculum takes on directly the question of foreign aid. For this audience, we also distribute a comic book and a slide show. Please write to us about these resources.

Other groups also offer invaluable tools for reaching young people on such global issues as poverty and hunger. We have included a few of those with which we are most familiar.

The Next Step: Linking Up

Alone we can accomplish little. When we join with others, not only do our actions have greater impact, but our energy and hope are buoyed. The list of periodicals and organizations that follows is hardly exhaustive. Fortunately, there are many more citizens' initiatives related to the issues this book raises than we could possibly include. So, we apologize in advance to all those groups that space limitation would not permit us to include.

For those working specifically on Central America, we recommend the exhaustive guide (with over 1,000 groups listed) which is published by the Central America Resource Center in Austin, listed below.

PERIODICALS

Africa News, P.O. Box 3851, Durham, NC 27702

Cultural Survival, 11 Divinity St., Cambridge, MA 02138

Food Monitor, World Hunger Year, 350 Broadway, Suite 209, New York, NY 10013

Multinational Monitor, P.O. Box 19405, Washington, DC 20036

NACLA Report on the Americas, 151 W. 19th St., New York, NY 10011

The National Catholic Reporter, P.O. Box 419281, Kansas City, MO 64141

New Internationalist, 74A High St., Wallingford, Berkshire, England

Seeds, 222 East Lake Dr., Decatur, GA 30030

World Policy Journal, World Policy Institute, 777 United Nations Plaza, New York, NY 10017

ORGANIZATIONS WORKING TO CHANGE U.S.
FOREIGN POLICY *(Most of these groups also publish regular newsletters and reports.)*

Africa Faith and Justice Network, 1233 Lawrence St. NE, Washington, DC 20017, 202-832-3412

American Committee on Africa/Africa Fund, 198 Broadway, New York, NY 10038, 212-962-1210

American Friends Service Committee, 1501 Cherry St., Philadelphia, PA 19102, 215-241-7000

Bread for the World, 802 Rhode Island Ave. NE, Washington, DC 20018, 202-269-0200

Center for Defense Information, 1500 Massachusetts Ave. NW, Washington, DC 20005, 202-862-0700

Center for International Policy, 236 Massachusetts Ave. NE, Suite 505, Washington, DC 20002, 202-544-4666

Center for National Security Studies, 122 Maryland Ave. NE, Washington, DC 20002, 202-544-5380

Center of Concern, 3700 13th St. NE, Washington, DC 20017, 202-635-2757

Central American Historical Institute, Intercultural Center, Georgetown University, Washington, DC 20057, 202-625-8246 (An excellent source for information on Nicaragua).

Central America Resource Center *(Guide to Central America Groups)* P.O. Box 2327, Austin, TX 78768, 512-476-9841

Clergy and Laity Concerned, 198 Broadway, Room 302, New York, NY 10038, 212-964-6730

Coalition for a New Foreign and Military Policy, 712 G St. SE, Washington, DC 20003, 202-546-8400

Committee for Health Rights in Central America, 513 Valencia St., Room 6, San Francisco, CA 94110, 415-431-7760

Committee in Solidarity with the People of El Salvador (CISPES), P.O. Box 12056, Washington, DC 20005, 202-393-3370

Development Group for Alternative Policies, 2200 19th St. NW, #206, Washington, DC 20009, 202-332-1600

Free South Africa Movement/TransAfrica, 545 8th St. SE, Washington, DC 20003, 202-547-2550

Guatemala News and Information Bureau, P.O. Box 28594, Oakland, CA 94604, 415-835-0810

Honduras Information Center, 1 Summer St., Somerville, MA 02143, 617-625-7220

Institute for Food and Development Policy (Food First), 145 Ninth St., San Francisco, CA 94103, 415-864-8555

Institute for Policy Studies, 1901 Q St. NW, Washington, DC 20009, 202-234-9382

Interfaith Action for Economic Justice, 110 Maryland Ave. NE, Washington, DC 20002, 202-543-2800

International Center for Development Policy, 731 8th St. SE, Washington, DC 20003, 202-547-3800

Mobilization for Survival, 853 Broadway, Room 418, New York, NY 10003, 212-533-0008

National Network in Solidarity with the Nicaraguan People, 2025 I St. NW, Suite 212, Washington, DC 20006, 202-223-2328

National Network in Solidarity with the People of Guatemala, 1314 14th St. NW, #515, Washington, DC 20005, 202-483-0050

Neighbor to Neighbor, 2940 16th St., San Francisco, CA 94103, 415-621-3711

Philippine Resource Center, Box 40090, Berkeley, CA 94704, 415-548-1546

The Resource Center, P.O. Box 4506, Albuquerque, NM 87196, 505-266-5009

Resources for Development and Democracy, 17119 Old Baltimore Road, Olney, MD 20832, 301-774-4669

Washington Office on Africa, 110 Maryland Ave. NE, Washington, DC 20002, 202-546-7961

Washington Office on Haiti, 110 Maryland Ave. NE, Washington, DC 20002, 202-543-7095

Washington Office on Latin America, 110 Maryland Ave. NE, Washington, DC 20002, 202-544-8045

GROUPS SPONSORING THIRD WORLD EDUCATIONAL TOURS

African American Heritage Study Association, 120 South La Salle St., Suite 1144, Chicago, IL 60003, 312-443-0920

Center for Global Service and Education, Augsburg College, 731 21st Ave. South, Minneapolis, MN 55454, 612-330-1159

Food First Reality Tours, 145 Ninth St., San Francisco, CA 94103, 415-864-8555

Our Developing World, 13004 Paseo Presada, Saratoga, CA 95070, 408-379-4431

Seeds Study Tours, 222 East Lake Drive, Decatur, GA 30030, 404-378-3566

Tropical Tours, 141 East 44th St., Suite 409, New York, NY 10017, 212-599-1441

World Neighbors, 5116 North Portland Ave., Oklahoma City, OK 73112, 405-946-3333

DIRECT AID GROUPS   *(For the many groups involved in direct aid to Central America, see the guide published by the Central America Resource Center, above.)*

Grassroots International, P.O. Box 312, Cambridge, MA 02139, 617-497-9180

Oxfam America, 115 Broadway, Boston, MA 02116, 617-482-1211

Pueblo to People, 5218 Chenevert, Houston, TX 77004, 713-523-1197

Unitarian Universalist Service Committee, 78 Beacon St., Boston, MA 02108, 617-742-2120

ORGANIZATIONS PROVIDING GLOBAL EDUCATION MATERIALS

Center for Teaching International Relations, Graduate School of International Studies, University of Denver, Denver, CO 80208, 303-871-3101

Educators for Social Responsibility, 3 Garden St., Cambridge, MA 02138, 617-492-1764

Global Perspectives in Education Network (GPIEN), 218 East 18th St., New York, NY 10003, 212-475-0850

Immaculate Heart College Center, 10951 West Pico Blvd., Suite 2021, Los Angeles, Ca 90064, 213-470-2293

Institute for Food and Development Policy (Food First), 145 Ninth St., San Francisco, CA 94103, 415-864-8555

Institute for Peace and Justice, 4144 Lindell St., #400, St. Louis, MO 63108, 314-533-4445

Office on Global Education, Church World Service, 2115 North Charles St., Baltimore, MD 21218, 301-727-6101

Oxfam America, 115 Broadway, Boston, MA 02116, 617-482-1221

Index